Cults in North America

Cults in North America

EARL SCHIPPER

CONTEMPORARY DISCUSSION SERIES

BAKER BOOK HOUSE

Grand Rapids, Michigan 49506

ISBN: 0-8010-8212-9

Printed in the United States of America

Contents

Cults in North America

1

What Is a Cult?

When asked to define the word *cult*, many people immediately think of young people selling carnations at airports, or religious fanatics standing on street corners passing out literature or going door-to-door preaching their beliefs. Some people identify cult members as people who reject blood transfusions, don't believe in medical treatment, refuse to salute the flag, or commit themselves to a voluntary two-year mission assignment.

A leader at a youth retreat gave participants the following description and instructed them to identify the religious group the person came from.

He goes out preaching whenever and wherever he can—Saturdays, Sundays, on street corners, in churches, especially in the larger cities. More than once he has spent time in jail because of religious disturbances caused by his unorthodox views. To support himself, he has a part-time job, but he spends most of his time preaching. In fact, he remains single because he wants no earthly obligations to keep him from preaching, since he's convinced the end is near.

The young people answered, "a Moonie," "a Jehovah's Witness," "a member of Hare Krishna," and "a member of the Children of God commune." Actually, the person described was the apostle Paul! The participants correctly observed that many stereotypes we hold about cult members apply to the apostle Paul as well. Further discussion revealed that the young people assumed that cult members are religious fanatics who aggressively seek to lure converts into their cult, and who share a rigid isolation from the world.

What Is a Cult?

The religious groups we will examine are usually referred to as cults in books of this nature. However, we will avoid using this troublesome term in the chapters that follow for one compelling reason. Although the word *cult* denotes a religious group that has deviated from traditional, orthodox Christianity, the word connotes a religious group that is characterized by unacceptable, bizarre practices.

To many people, the word *cult* connotes a religious group that practices brainwashing, recruits members by deceiving them, and is controlled by a powerful leader who abuses power (such as the infamous Rev. Jim Jones, who led members of the People's Temple to a mass suicide in Guyana).

While certain religious groups may, in fact, exhibit bizarre, unacceptable behavior, it would be unfair to associate some of the religious groups we will study with these outrageous practices. For this reason, we will use the word *cult* in this chapter to mean only that which it denotes; we will avoid its use in subsequent chapters because of what it connotes. Let's attempt to clarify our understanding of cults by asking some questions.

Aren't cult members radical religious fanatics? If by "fanatic" we mean that cult members show a high level of personal commitment, yes. Christian leaders often admire the radical commitment of cult members and cite them as examples to Christians. But many evangelical Christians display a radical commitment as well. Literal obedience to Christ's words, "Anyone who loves his father or mother more than me is not worthy of me" (Matt. 10:37), has produced scores of Christians who demonstrate radical personal commitment. Christian groups such as the Koinonia Community at Americus, Georgia, demonstrate radical Christian commitment to racial justice and communal life. We should also remember that cults, like orthodox churches, contain nominal, less committed members. Apparently, radical followers are not unique to cults.

Don't all cults use an aggressive evangelistic approach? Some do, some don't. The First Unification Church uses methods of evangelism which have brought accusations of brainwashing, but Mormons and Jehovah's Witnesses, who evangelize door-to-door, demonstrate courtesy in their contacts with prospective members. Christian

Science relies on reading rooms at strategic locations for inquirers or prospective members, an approach which is anything but aggressive. In addition, many orthodox Christian churches and mission outreach programs exhibit aggressive methods. Clearly, aggressive evangelism isn't a characteristic unique to cults.

Isn't it true that cults attempt to lure orthodox Christians away from churches? It certainly is. In fact, some of the most productive contacts made by the cults fall into two categories: inactive church members who have religious sensitivity and a nominal religious affiliation, but lack an adequate knowledge of Bible teaching; and Christians who attend church but feel unfulfilled spiritually and socially.

But the cults also attempt to win the unchurched. For example, Jehovah's Witnesses often make evangelistic calls on Sunday morning, while churchgoers are away from home, in order to reach the unchurched. But attempting to lure Christians away from orthodox churches is not unique to the cults. Many forces, such as materialism, communism, hedonism, and an infinite list of other idols, lure people away. What distinguishes the cults from these *isms* is that the cults use the names of God and Jesus Christ in their attempts to recruit members: ". . . to deceive even the elect—if that were possible" (Matt. 24:24). This intention of the cults enhances the need for Christians to study the origins and beliefs of the cults.

Aren't cults usually isolated from others, somewhat paranoid? This is often true. Members of cults often feel that the entire world, including orthodox churches, is against them, or that they alone have the truth. In the First Unification Church, for example, new converts are kept in the "protective custody of the cult"; previous social and family relationships are severed to the point of nearly complete isolation. To a lesser degree, members of other cults develop extremely intense ties, and the convert's life is reoriented within the cult. To support these ties, severe penalties are established to punish members who leave the group, often including total rejection and personal shame. Defecting cult members often tell how cult leaders required that they sacrifice personal identification by restricting social relations and demanding strict allegiance to the cult's beliefs and practices. Two factors, however, explain why isolation and paranoia are not criteria of cults.

First, cults often originate and exist in a very hostile environment. Early Mormons, for example, experienced shameful persecutions, often at the hands of angry, abusive people, Christian and non-Christian alike. Every cult we will study has encountered suspicion, distrust, disapproval, and hostility. Quite predictably, cult members are driven to each other and develop intense personal ties as a defense against external disapproval and hostility. But this tendency to isolation should be understood as a sociological phenomenon, not as a unique characteristic of the cults.

Second, many Christian denominations exhibit the same characteristics. For example, the Amish, the Mennonites, and the New Apostolic Church of

Canada all isolate themselves, fear the world, and practice passionate internal loyalties. Early immigrant churches demonstrated the same characteristics. Apparently, segregation is not unique to the cults.

Here it would be helpful to distinguish cults from sects. A sect accepts traditional Christian beliefs, acknowledges the sole authority of the Bible, and is close to orthodox Christianity, but emphasizes one particular aspect of Christian truth. A cult accepts some authority or source for truth outside the Scriptures. Therefore, the Mormons, who accept scriptures other than the Bible, are a cult; whereas the Amish, who accept the Bible but emphasize separation from the world, are a sect.

Basic Differences

Features distinguishing the cults from orthodox churches are far more significant than the lifestyle and practices we have just examined. Christians would be relieved if cults were distinguished only by harmless idiosyncrasies or superficial differences in religious practice. The differences are much more basic, affecting the biblical understanding of God, salvation, and revelation. If Christians minimize these differences, or regard them as shallow and unimportant, they fail to see the spiritual peril inherent in the teachings of the cults. Let's examine some of the most fundamental dissimilarities of the cults. What basic beliefs or approaches to truth characterize the cults?

Cults reinterpret or deny the deity of Christ. To

affirm the deity of Christ, Christians cite the following biblical teachings.

1. Jesus Christ was an incarnation of God.

In the beginning was the Word, and the Word was with God, and the Word was God. He was with God in the beginning. Through him all things were made; without him nothing was made that has been made. [John 1:1–3]

"The virgin will be with child and will give birth to a son, and they will call him Immanuel"—which means, "God with us." [Matt. 1:23]

2. Jesus Christ is equal to God.

Your attitude should be the same as that of Christ Jesus: Who, being in very nature God, did not consider equality with God something to be grasped, but made himself nothing, taking the very nature of a servant, being made in human likeness. [Phil. 2:5–7]

Although many more passages could be cited, these two statements supply the basic contrast between the teachings of orthodox Christianity and those of the cults. Cults do not, as is sometimes alleged, deny the divinity of Christ. Each cult we will study teaches His *divinity*, but denies His *deity*. As we will notice, this denial of the deity of Christ contains a logical denial of the Trinity. Therefore, as we study individual cults, we will focus on their teaching about the person and role of Jesus Christ and the nature of God.

Cults offer an unbiblical basis for salvation. Recall what the Bible teaches about salvation:

1. Salvation is by faith, not works. "For it is by grace you have been saved, through faith—and this is not from yourselves, it is the gift of God—not by works, so that no one can boast" (Eph. 2:8–9).
2. Salvation by faith comes through Jesus Christ exclusively. "Salvation is found in no one else, for there is no other name under heaven given to men by which we must be saved" (Acts 4:12).
3. Salvation by faith through Christ has been accomplished once, for all time. ". . . But now he [Jesus] has appeared once for all at the end of the ages to do away with sin by the sacrifice of himself" (Heb. 9:26b).
4. The biblical plan of salvation will never be superseded, will never be obsolete, and will never require elaboration. ". . . some people are throwing you into confusion and are trying to pervert the gospel of Christ. But even if we or an angel from heaven should preach a gospel other than the one we preached to you, let him be eternally condemned" (Gal. 1:7–8).

In contrast with biblical teaching, cult teachings minimize the work of Jesus and emphasize human works in salvation. Christ's work, according to the cults, gives each person the opportunity to be saved. Christ is needed, but not all-sufficient, for salvation. In this way, the importance of Christ is reduced from what the Bible teaches

What then do the cults teach about how we can be saved?

Each cult emphasizes some form of salvation by works. Although Christ makes salvation possible, cults teach that a person must earn one's own, personal salvation by obedience to God's will as it is interpreted and taught by the cult. As we study each cult, we will focus our attention on the role of Christ and the importance of human works in salvation.

Cults claim a new revelation from God which either restores a lost biblical gospel or teaches truths in addition to the Bible. To understand this better, let's briefly examine how Christians accept the Bible.

1. The Bible is God's revelation to humankind.

I want you to know, brothers, that the gospel I preach is not something that man made up. I did not receive it from any man, nor was I taught it; rather, I received it by revelation from Jesus Christ. [Gal. 1:11–12]

2. The Bible is inspired and infallible.

All scripture is God-breathed and is useful for teaching, rebuking, correcting and training in righteousness, so that the man of God may be thoroughly equipped for every good work. [II Tim. 3:16–17]

3. The Bible is God's complete revelation.

17

I warn everyone who hears the words of the prophecy of this book: If anyone adds anything to them, God will add to him the plagues described in this book. And if anyone takes words away from this book of prophecy, God will take away from him his share in the tree of life and in the holy city, which are described in this book. [Rev. 22:18–19]

4. The Holy Spirit who inspired the Bible has preserved the true gospel.

But when he, the Spirit of truth, comes, he will guide you into all truth. He will not speak on his own; he will speak only what he hears. . . . [John 16:13]

In contrast to the Christian understanding of the Bible, each cult teaches that it has received some revelation or disclosure from God that orthodox churches do not have. Cult teachings reveal two explanations of why and how this happened.

Some cults maintain that God removed the truth from the earth at the time of Constantine because the church had become a political institution and perverted the purity of the gospel. After an extended absence of the true gospel from the earth, God ultimately revealed the "restored" or "pure" gospel to the founders and religious leaders of the respective cults. In each cult, the founder claimed he or she was given a new version or new insight which restored the original biblical truth. What characterized these new revelations was their purpose to restore or reestablish the true biblical gospel.

Another belief, sometimes coexisting with a belief in a restored Bible, claims that God continues to reveal Himself directly and supernaturally. Mormons, for example, earnestly believe that the leader of their church is a prophet of God who receives *continuing* revelations from God, as have all previous leaders of their cult. Because cult members believe that God has given new revelations in one or both of these ways, they believe they have been singled out as exclusive recipients of God's true and complete gospel.

Cults and Scripture

Evangelical Christians often deplore cult members' willing acceptance of new revelations that supposedly supersede the Bible. But we must not allow these feelings to obscure the fact that the religious groups we will study accept the Bible as inspired revelation, even though they reinterpret Scripture and subordinate it to newer revelations. Realizing the power of God's Word, Christians should rejoice that God has not left the cults without witness.

For many cult members, the power of the Bible has exposed the false systems and unbiblical teachings of their groups. Today there are organizations of ex-Mormons, ex-Jehovah's Witnesses, ex-Moonies, and former members of many other groups. The lives of these people have been powerfully changed by the Word of God. Some of them have written informative, revealing, and helpful books about the cults.

Furthermore, cults change over the years. As

the witness of God's Word remains within deviant religious groups, their teachings sometimes become more and more like the teachings of traditional Christianity. The Mormon church recently ended nearly 150 years of unbiblical discrimination as a new revelation granted blacks equal treatment as "one in Christ." The Christian Science church has shown an interest in recent years in exchanging dialogue with main-line Protestant churches in order to define and lessen differences between Christian Science and traditional Christianity.

A Definition

Having analyzed what distinguishes a cult from orthodox Christian denominations, we should be able to do two things: to define what we mean by a cult, and to designate the most pertinent teachings of the cults before we study each individually.

We can define a cult by listing the three distinctive features of cults: an unbiblical view of salvation, denial of the deity of Christ, and a claim of new revelation. Putting these together, we may define a cult as "a religious group that claims a new or restored revelation from God, including an unbiblical basis for salvation and rejection of the deity of Christ." Comparing our definition with another widely used definition, we will find basic agreement. Often a cult is defined as "any religion regarded as unorthodox or spurious by traditional, historical Christianity." Essentially, this definition confirms our conclusion but our definition specifies how cult teachings differ from those of historical, biblical Christianity. This is helpful for organizing what you learn about the cults.

As we examine the origins and beliefs of the cults in subsequent chapters, we will focus on these topics: the nature of God, the person and role of Christ, the way of salvation, and divine revelations in addition to the Bible. These topics will guide but not limit our study.

More than a thousand cults have started in the past twenty-five years. Many originated in North America and spread to Europe, Africa, and Asia. Others have remained localized in geographical areas. Because of their diversity and mobility, selecting religious groups to study is a problem.

Two questions helped us determine which cults to include. First, "Which cults have proved most appealing and popular since their founding?" Second, "Which cults will readers confront most frequently?" Using these criteria, we limited the number to five: Mormonism, Jehovah's Witnesses, Christian Science (all of which arose in America during the 1800s and have gained significant numbers of converts), First Unification Church, and The Way International (which have appeared only recently, but have quickly gained converts, especially among young people).

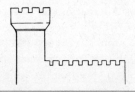

2

Jehovah's Witnesses

The Watch Tower Bible and Tract Society is the corporate body of the Jehovah's Witness organization. The Jehovah's Witness magazine, *The Watchtower*, published by the society, is distributed by the millions weekly.

Jehovah's Witnesses, also called The Watchtower Society, receive a great deal of unrequested publicity. From time to time newspapers feature stories with headlines such as, "Parents Object—Judge Orders Transfusion." Such articles report the condition of a sick child whose parents refuse to permit a blood transfusion, even though medical doctors warn that failure to act could take the child's life. To account for the parents' refusal, the article explains that Jehovah's Witnesses believe that the infusion of another creature's blood into one's body is strictly forbidden by God (see Lev. 3:17; Deut. 12:27). They believe this so strongly that a devout Jehovah's Witness would rather die than disobey God by having a blood transfusion.

Newspapers also report the persecution of Jehovah's Witnesses in other countries, especially Russia and some African nations. Because members must disavow allegiance to any government, whatever the country, the Witnesses often meet resistance and antagonism. A few countries, such as Australia and Liberia, have banned the group entirely.

You have very likely been contacted by Jehovah's Witnesses, perhaps without realizing it. They often stand on busy sidewalks, distributing copies of a magazine called *Awake!* Or they may have come to your door with religious literature, asking for a chance to explain the blessings that will come to those who are prepared for the coming Kingdom of God. Although there are fewer than 1.5 million members worldwide, Jehovah's Witnesses, through persistent missionary work and unusual practices, have become widely known in many countries. People notice a religious group whose members refuse to vote, reject blood transfusions, remain seated during the national anthem, reject the cross as a religious symbol, would go to jail rather than serve in the military, and forbid their children to celebrate birthdays, Christmas, or Easter.

Who are these people? Where did the Jehovah's Witnesses come from? To answer these questions, we must go back to the eastern United States of more than a hundred years ago.

The Origin of Jehovah's Witnesses

The Religious Climate

During the mid-1800s, a popular movement swept through Protestant churches in the eastern

United States. Called "Second Adventism" because it focused on the second coming or advent of Jesus Christ, this movement created a surge of interest in biblical prophecy. Under the dynamic leadership of William Miller, Bible conferences advancing a strict literal interpretation of prophecy became very popular. Although Second Adventists disagreed on some details, they insisted on four basic beliefs which resulted from their interpretation of prophecy:

1. There will be no everlasting hell or eternal punishment of sinners.
2. Jehovah has a plan to restore godly people to everlasting life on this earth.
3. The end of the world is about to happen.
4. When Jesus comes again, He will resurrect the righteous, judge the wicked, and restore this earth to its original perfection. Once the earth is restored, Christ will reign for one thousand years. After that, earth will be the believers' eternal home.

Sharp differences arose about *when* Christ would return. Bible study convinced the Second Adventists, led by Miller, that Christ would return on or before April 18, 1844. As the date approached, many of these adventists confidently sold their earthly possessions and prepared to meet Jesus. When the advent failed to materialize, many followers became disenchanted. But some remained loyal to Miller, who was undaunted. What had happened, he claimed, was that Christ had returned in some spiritual way, not a physical way, as they had expected. To Miller and his followers, the year 1844 marked the beginning of the end, but the literal physical return of Christ would take place over a period of years. These prophecies caused yet another splinter group.

The splinter group claimed that Miller had miscalculated the date for Christ's return. Re-examination of the prophecies of Daniel and Revelation indicated to them that the year should have been 1874. One splinter-group congregation was located in Allegheny, Pennsylvania. One evening in 1868, just six years before the anticipated return of Christ, a bewildered and disillusioned seventeen-year-old agnostic sat alone in a pew. He was Charles Taze Russell, a sensitive, inquiring ex-Christian.

The Life of Charles Taze Russell

Charles Russell was born in 1852 in Allegheny, Pennsylvania, where his father ran a men's clothing store. Work in the family store prevented Charles from getting much formal education, and he left school at the age of fourteen, having completed the seventh grade. Brought up in his parents' Presbyterian church, Charles developed serious doubts and extraordinary fears.

Charles' doubts centered on two doctrines he had been taught: eternal punishment and predestination. We can only speculate on the connection between his doubts and the emotional fear of hell which he exhibited. As a young boy he scribbled warnings about hell on the sidewalks of Allegheny. After Charles had spent years in troubled discussion and emotional struggle, his doubts evolved into disbelief and skepticism. By the time he was seventeen, he had lost faith in churches, distrusted all denominations, and disbelieved the Bible. When Charles wandered into the Second Adventist congregation in Allegheny that year, he was an agnostic, doubting that it was possible to know any truth about God.

That night Charles listened intently to the teachings of the Second Adventists. He was especially fascinated and captivated by the precise way in which Bible prophecies explained what had happened and was happening in world history. According to the adventists, the intriguing prophecies of Daniel, Ezekiel, and Revelation disclosed the ways great empires of the past and present rose and fell, fulfilling exactly the ancient prophecies. Even years, months, and days mentioned in Bible prophecies corresponded to historical dates and periods of known history. Charles's hungry mind absorbed the logical, coherent interpretation of prophecy, but for Charles Russell the true value of that night lay in his rekindled belief in the divine inspiration of the Bible. This new confidence would make him a lifetime student of the Bible.

By the time he was twenty, Charles Russell had organized a Bible-study group with five other students. During this time, Russell attained absolute confidence that he had discovered the true meaning of the Bible. Even though he had no knowledge of the original languages in which the Bible was written, and although he had no qualifying education, he boldly claimed possession of new

27

insights which would restore biblical truth to the world. An interesting anecdote illustrates his confidence.

In his early twenties, Russell invited all the ministers from Pittsburgh and Allegheny to a public meeting. The purpose of the meeting was to educate these misguided ministers with the "new light" which God had restored to the world. The date and time were widely advertised, Russell carefully prepared his revolutionary lecture, and the hall was made ready. Not one minister showed up. Critics claim that Russell was totally embittered by this experience and hated all denominations from that day until his death.

By the age of twenty-four, Charles Russell had become the pastor of the tiny Bible-study group. He sold his interest in the men's clothing store and spent the next forty years spreading his new-found religious beliefs by lecturing and writing. By the time he died in 1916, Russell had systematized the Witnesses' teachings into a fundamental set of doctrines which later became the basis for the *New World Translation* of the Bible. Many doctrinal refinements have come about during the leadership of his successors, Judge Rutherford, Nathan Knorr, and the current president, Frederick Franz, but the basic beliefs of Charles Russell remain deeply ingrained in the Watchtower Society. He condemned all translations of the Bible as corrupt; rejected the teachings of all denominations, claiming the orthodox churches belonged to the ecclesiastical division of Satan's kingdom; denied the deity and physical resurrection of Jesus Christ; disbelieved the existence of hell or eternal punishment; and claimed the ability to predict precisely when Christ would return. As we review the Witnesses' beliefs, these teachings will surface repeatedly.

The Beliefs and Practices of Jehovah's Witnesses

The Nature of God

If there is one topic the Witnesses enjoy discussing with Christians, it is the nature of God. Witnesses regard the Christian understanding of God as extremely offensive and as proof that Satan controls all Christian churches, Protestant and Catholic alike. What exactly is the Witnesses' concept of God?

Jehovah's Witnesses insist that only the name Jehovah *be used for God.* Jehovah is God's personal name, which sets Him apart from the "counterfeit gods" of the world's religions. The name *God*, they say, is nothing more than a title, like "president," "king," or "judge." To address the God of the Bible, one must use His name, Jehovah. Doesn't the Bible, they ask, instruct us to use only His personal name? "Before me there was no God formed, and after me there continued to be none. I—I am Jehovah, and besides me there is no savior" (Isa. 43:10–11, NWT). Witnesses believe that Christians who neglect to use the name *Jehovah* have corrupted His name and disgraced His honor. (See also Ps. 83:18 and Isa. 44:8 in the American Standard Version.)

Jehovah's Witnesses repel any notion of the Trinity, even though they share the Christian view that God is a Spirit, that He created the world and rules all things, and that He deserves all praise and glory. Neither the word *trinity* nor the idea of the Trinity, they allege, is found anywhere in the Bible. In their missionary contacts, Witnesses encounter many Christians who express surprise on learning that the word *trinity* is not in the Bible. The following reconstruction of a Jehovah's Witnesses' training session reveals how they are taught to take advantage of this surprise to refute the Christian belief in the Trinity.

Question: Where did the word *trinity* come from?

Answer: It is not found in the Bible and was not used in official church creeds until the Council of Nicaea in A.D. 325. In command of this church council was a Roman emperor, Constantine. He was the culprit who introduced the idea of a trinity to make Christianity more appealing to the polytheistic Romans and Greeks. The idea was borrowed from the ancient pagan beliefs of the Babylonians, who worshiped more than one trinity of gods.

Question: Is the idea of a trinity found in the Bible?

Answer: When Jesus was on earth, he certainly did not claim to be equal to his Father, for he said there were some things that neither he nor the angels knew, but only God knew (Mark 13:32). He prayed to his Father for help (Luke 22:41–42). And he said, "The Father is greater than I am" (John 14:28b, NWT). Furthermore, Paul wrote in

1 Corinthians 11:3, "... the head of every man is the Christ; in turn the head of a woman is the man; in turn the head of the Christ is God" (NWT).

If someone answers, "But Jesus said, 'I and the Father are one'" (John 10:30, NWT), we reply like this: Yes, but this doesn't suggest a trinity, only a duality. What he meant is identical to the expression he used when he prayed regarding his followers, '... that they may be one just as we are one' (John 17:22, NWT). If someone replies that John 1:1 teaches that Jesus, the Word, is one with God, call their attention to John 1:18a, which says, "No man has seen God at any time ..." (NWT). Yet the people saw Jesus Christ, so he must not have been God. The correct translation of John 1:1 must be, "the Word was with God, and the Word was divine," or "was a god." As for the Holy Spirit—it is not a person, but an active force. John the Baptist said that Jesus would baptize with the Holy Spirit, even as John had baptized with water (Matt. 3:11). Now, water is not a person, so the Holy Spirit isn't a person either. On Pentecost, the disciples were filled with God's active force, not with a person (Acts 2:4, 33).

Question: Is the trinity reasonable?

Answer: When Jesus prayed, "... yet, not as I will, but as you will" (Matt. 26:39, NWT), did he mean "Not as *I* will, but as *I* will?" This doesn't make sense. Furthermore, Jesus was in the grave for three days. If Jesus was God, who ruled the universe during that time? And what about the Holy Spirit? Can a person be poured out on another person? Can people be baptized with a person? These things are possible only if the Holy Spirit is an active force.

31

The conclusions of the Jehovah's Witnesses are that the trinity originated in pagan religions, the trinity is not biblical, and the trinity is not reasonable.

Jehovah's Witnesses' rejection of the Trinity results from their rejection of Christ's deity and the personal nature of the Holy Spirit. Before we examine more closely the Witnesses' beliefs about Jesus Christ, let's examine how they believe God must be honored.

Jehovah's Witnesses insist that Jehovah alone may receive honor and praise. According to the Witnesses, the Bible warns against giving credit or honor to any person, nation, or institution, because this detracts from the honor due only to Jehovah (Jer. 17:5–7). A holiday or special commemoration which gives credit to any creature displeases Jehovah (Acts 10:25–26). Witnesses disapprove of three categories of celebration.

1. Birthdays. Celebrating birthdays exalts *people*, making them the center of attention, which detracts from Jehovah. The only two birthdays mentioned in the Bible are those of rulers who followed false religions: Pharaoh of Egypt and Herod Antipas. If we seek to please Jehovah and avoid pagan customs, say the Witnesses, we must not celebrate birthdays.

2. Special days which honor people. The Witnesses contend that days set aside in honor of persons, living or dead, displease Jehovah, because such celebrations encourage us to credit people—not Jehovah—for human prog-

ress and earthly blessings. Therefore Jehovah's Witnesses must ignore days such as Martin Luther King Day, the queen's birthday, and Veterans' Day.
3. Holidays which honor nations or worldly institutions. It is an offensive custom, according to the Witnesses, to credit human organizations for progress, since Jehovah alone deserves the credit. Holidays such as Dominion Day, United Nations Day, Independence Day, and Memorial Day detract from Jehovah's honor.

The Witnesses also believe it is wrong to celebrate Easter or Christmas, although the reasons differ from those previously given. These celebrations should be avoided because they allegedly have pagan—not Christian—origins. By avoiding all these celebrations, the Witnesses testify that they are freed from earthly obligations in order to follow the right path of total devotion to Jehovah.

Teachings About Christ

Because the Jehovah's Witnesses' understanding of Jesus Christ is defined by their understanding of Christ's place in God's plan of redemption, we will divide our study into two parts: first, the person of Christ; second, His role in salvation.

The person of Christ. According to the literature of the Jehovah's Witnesses, Jesus existed in three stages. In his first stage, Jesus was the very first spirit creature, created by Jehovah and given the name *Michael*. Together with Jehovah, Jesus/ Michael created other spirit creatures, but Jesus Christ is the first, the only begotten son of Jehovah. Others were begotten by Jehovah and Michael. In his second stage, this spirit creature came to earth as Jesus of Nazareth, entirely and exclusively human. Born to Mary without the aid of an earthly father, he escaped the influence of original sin and was able to live a perfect, obedient life. As a perfect human being, Jesus gave his life as a payment for sin. In his third stage he was resurrected as a spirit creature, not a physically resurrected creature. Jesus returned to heaven and is now honored as Jehovah's Chief Son. When the present world order is destroyed, King Jesus will literally return to earth, resurrect 144,000 believers, and take them to heaven where they will reign eternally.

The idea of Jesus existing in three distinct phases raises several fundamental questions. First, was He divine? The Witnesses' definition of the meaning of the person of Christ is quite different from the view of historic Christianity. To them, He is divine in the limited sense of having come to earth from a pre-earth life as a spirit creature. The incarnation Russell explains as follows:

> Neither was Jesus a combination of the two natures, human and spiritual. The blending of two natures produces neither the one nor the other, but an imperfect, hybrid thing, which is obnoxious to the divine arrangement. When Jesus was in the flesh, He was a perfect human being; previous to

that He was a spiritual being; and since His resurrection He is a perfect spiritual being of the highest or Divine order.[1]

A second question relates to the resurrection of Christ. Did He experience a bodily resurrection? According to the Witnesses, Jesus was raised a spirit creature. What happened to His body is not known, although the Witnesses assume it did not decay and might be preserved somewhere as a memorial to God's love. The implications of this belief are staggering to the Christian: Jesus, according to the Witnesses' teaching, did not receive a glorified body, and did not take our human nature to heaven!

This raises a third, related question: What of the physical return of Christ? According to the Witnesses, Jesus' return is neither physical nor visible. In fact, they teach that Jesus returned in 1914, the year labeled the "end of the Gentile times." So to them Christ's return does not mean that He will return as a glorified Jesus Christ to earth. Rather, they believe that He has taken up His kingly rule toward the earth, that 1914 marked the beginning of a transitional period of preparation for the end time, and that the Kingdom of Jehovah has already begun.

The role of Christ. To understand how the Witnesses view the role Christ plays in salvation, we

1. As quoted by Rev. A. Wassink in *The Bible and Jehovah's Witnesses* (Grand Rapids: Faith, Prayer, and Tract League), p. 4.

must first outline the basic framework of their teaching about God's plan of redemption:

1. Jehovah created the heavens first, then Michael. Then, together with Michael, He created the angels.
2. Jehovah created the earth, assigning a task force of angels to assure that all worship and praise on earth would be directed only to Jehovah.
3. Disguising himself as a serpent, the leader of the task force seduced Adam and Eve to worship him because he became jealous as he listened every day to the praise given to Jehovah.
4. With other rebellious angels, the fallen angel Satan gained total control of the earth. The penalty of death hung over all creation.
5. Jehovah issued this challenge to Satan: "I'll give you 6,000 years to seduce the whole earth into worshiping you. If you fail, you and all fallen angels (demons) will be annihilated and I will have proven that I alone am Supreme."
6. Knowing Satan would fail, Jehovah initiated His plan to save the world. Most importantly, Jehovah wanted to give eternal life to some persons now condemned to eternal death. Satan agreed to release his grip of death on a certain number, but demanded a ransom payment—to have a chance to destroy Michael—after which Satan would remove the penalty of death for some of the condemned. In response, Jehovah sent Michael to earth in human form as a ransom paid to Satan. After

the death of Jesus, the man, Jehovah raised him from the dead as His Chief Son.

This view of Christ's death, called *the ransom atonement*, makes it possible for people to be saved; it provides an opportunity for the obedient of the earth to escape eternal death. Those who are saved fall into two categories: the first is the anointed class, who are the most obedient of all people since time began. Quoting Revelation 14:1–3, Jehovah's Witnesses believe that there will be 144,000 in the anointed class, who will rule in heaven with Christ. Sometimes called "the little flock" these redeemed began to reign with Jesus when He returned in 1914, but their number will be completed only at the end of the present world order. The "other sheep" are the many who join Jehovah's Kingdom and earn eternal life by obediently following the example of Jesus, the only perfect human being who ever lived.

The place of Jesus in the plan of redemption is this: Jesus' death was a human sacrifice, a ransom paid to Satan, removing the penalty of death and making it possible for some to earn salvation. Knowing this, we can anticipate the Witnesses' answer to the question, "How are we saved?"

The Way of Salvation

Although Jehovah's Witnesses favor describing Jesus as "the One through whom Jehovah blesses mankind," a review of their literature demonstrates heavy emphasis on works as the basis for salvation. Salvation, it is taught, is made possible

37

for us through Christ, but we must obtain eternal life by following the Way of Jehovah. But what precisely does this mean?

To follow the Way of Jehovah demands two commitments: "to get out of Babylon the Great and to follow Christ." To help us understand the first, a Witness would answer two pointed questions.

What or who is Babylon? It is a religious empire such as Christianity or any other which has been corrupted by pagan beliefs such as the Trinity, the existence of hell, and the immortality of the human soul and those who maintain celebrations rooted in the pagan practices of Babylon, such as Christmas and Easter.

What does it mean to "get out"? It means to repudiate pagan beliefs and customs and withdraw membership. Since the Jehovah's Witnesses have repudiated both pagan Babylon and pagan Christendom, a person must associate with this visible organization which honors Jehovah purely. By devout service to Jehovah through this visible organization, His people are trained and equipped to please Him and to obtain eternal life in His coming Kingdom.

In addition to leaving "Babylon the Great," Witnesses believe in following the example of Christ. In both personal and family life, the Witnesses often lead exemplary lives. As individuals, Witnesses seek to follow Jesus as closely as possible, and their moral code is very strict. They reject divorce and premarital sex, and they deny the desires of the flesh. They avoid reading pornographic books and magazines and viewing sexually oriented movies or television shows. They yearn to obey the Ten Commandments and Christ's command to love their fellow human beings (John 13:34). Because they are so committed to loving all people, Witnesses are conscientious objectors to war, even though their position has brought them harsh treatment. During World War II, many Witnesses were put in prison for refusing to take up weapons; in Germany they were placed in concentration camps. Witnesses equate the immorality of our time with the immorality which existed at the time of Noah; they anticipate a similar destruction of the world, an opinion which encourages them to remain separate and holy unto Jehovah.

Witnesses' family and social lives are guided by strict moral codes as well. Their leaders encourage them to build strong families, to respect marriage, to discipline their children, to be honest in business, and to avoid evils such as gambling, drunkenness, homosexuality, and neglect of the elderly and handicapped. Without question, their desire to imitate the obedience of Jesus produces lives and families of strong moral character.

What are the Witnesses' motives for leading obedient lives? In contrast to Christianity, which emphasizes an obedient life motivated by gratitude to God, the Witnesses emphasize the duty and reward of obedience. Rarely is their obedience and loyalty to God's will a grateful response for what God has already done. Rather, Witnesses believe that they will earn a place in the new earth as a reward for living an upright life. And their belief in the annihilation of the wicked encourages them to obey Jehovah out of fear. Clearly, Witnesses trust in the value of good works for their salvation.

The Bible

We have already reviewed how Charles Russell claimed unique insights which enabled him to interpret the Bible correctly, thus restoring the "pure gospel." We also noted that Russell's teachings became the basis for a new, allegedly correct, translation of the Bible called the *New World Translation*. But we have not yet examined the way the Witnesses use the Bible in their missionary contacts.

Although the Witnesses accept the Bible as God's Word, infallible and inspired, they are often accused of using Bible verses out of context to support their doctrines. Using information from William Stevenson's *The Inside Story of Jehovah's Witnesses,* we can construct the following illustration of the way Witnesses use the Bible. Mr. Stevenson's fourteen-year membership in the Witnesses gives credibility to this condensed conversation between a Witness and a prospective convert.

J.W.: Good morning. My name is John Roberts and we're with a group of Bible students calling in your neighborhood this morning. In these days of energy problems, drugs, and inflation, I'd like to brighten your day by showing you from the Bible how this world is going to get turned around. You could probably use a little good news, couldn't you?

Mrs. Smith: Nowadays you don't hear that much *good* news.

J.W.: Most everyone we meet is concerned about crime, delinquency, nuclear war—but did you know that all these things, according to the Bible, will pass away and something will take their place?

Mrs. Smith: That would be wonderful . . . if only it were true.

J.W.: Look at this verse from Revelation 21 in your Bible (RSV): "He [God] will dwell with them, and they shall be his people, and God himself will be with them; he will wipe away every tear from their eyes, and death shall be no more, neither shall there be mourning nor crying, nor pain anymore, for the former things have passed away." Sounds too good to be true, doesn't it?

Mrs. Smith: Well, yes, it does. But isn't that what heaven will be like?

J.W.: That's what many people think. But look at this Scripture. It tells us all this will happen on this very earth. "Yet a little while, and the wicked will be no more; though you look well at his place, he will not be there" (Ps. 37:10). See how clearly this shows that the wicked will be removed from the earth?

Mrs. Smith: It does seem to say that.

J.W.: And notice the next verse. "But the meek shall possess the land, and delight themselves in abundant prosperity." You see, God has promised that this present order will pass away and be replaced by something very special right here on earth. The Bible even tells us that all people will be youthful.

Mrs. Smith: That's hard to believe.

J.W.: Here it is in Job 33:25, ". . . let his flesh become

41

fresh with youth; let him return to the days of his youthful vigor. . . ." How does that sound to you? Wouldn't you like to grow young instead of old?

Mrs. Smith: Wouldn't everyone? But I don't know, this all sounds quite different.

J.W.: I know it sounds far-fetched. When I first heard it, I thought the same thing. But I can show you from the Bible how it is possible for you and your family to survive this present world and be part of the new kingdom God has promised *in our lifetime.* I'd like your permission to come back next week. You get out your Bible and I'll get out my Bible and we'll take less than a half hour to study.

Mrs. Smith: Well, the only night we have free is Friday.

J.W.: You name the night. I'll be happy to plan on Friday night. After all, Mrs. Smith, if you find out that it's wrong, you've lost nothing. If you find out it's true, think of what a marvelous future you have to look forward to!

Jehovah's Witnesses are notorious for taking Bible verses out of context to support their beliefs. They remove texts from their settings and give them unintended meanings. The statement from Job 33:25, for example, is a passing comment of Elihu to Job. The Witnesses consider it a prophecy about the coming kingdom. And they interpret the words of the psalmist as predictions about the twentieth century—in a psalm of passionate response to pressing details of his personal life (Ps. 37). Obviously, such use of Bible verses fails to consider the historical setting and natural meaning of the words, selecting them to fit the preconceived notions and religious biases of the Witnesses.

World Events and the Future

According to the Witnesses, thirty-nine events must occur before the end of the present age. These include earthquakes, floods, famines, efforts to unite all nations (the United Nations), and war in the Middle East. Since these and the rest of the thirty-nine events have occurred or are occurring, the Witnesses live in anticipation of seeing the end. But what exactly do they expect?

1. The complete end of wickedness will occur in the war at Har-Magedon (*Armageddon* in the Bible), which will be a nuclear war in the Middle East.
2. On one side will be Christian nations, non-Christian nations, Communist nations, Catholics and Protestants, and the heathen. On the other side will be the true followers of Jehovah, both the anointed and the other sheep.
3. In a terrible battle in which Jehovah destroys the nations of earth with a holy vengeance, billions will die, destroyed by violent disturbances of nature, cloudbursts, floods, hail, and storms of fire.
4. The anointed will join others to be with Jesus in heaven. These are the 144,000 who have been most obedient throughout the ages.
5. Other faithful followers, the other sheep, will assist Jehovah in cleaning up the earth. Those who have died without a chance to know the truth about Jehovah will be resurrected and taught the right way. This period will last for a thousand years.

6. At the end of the millennium, all who reject Jehovah will be annihilated. There is no hell, no place of everlasting punishment. All who are alive will remain on the restored, Edenlike earth forever.

The official Witness magazine, *The Watchtower*, has predicted that the world would end in 1914, 1918, 1925, 1941, and 1975. These predictions have repeatedly proved embarrassing. After the latest prediction failed, a large number of Witnesses became disillusioned and left the church. These former members, including a nephew of President Franz, were disfellowshiped, a practice that resembles excommunication but also requires that all Jehovah's Witnesses, even family, regard the disfellowshiped as dead.

The Organization of Jehovah's Witnesses

The headquarters of the Jehovah's Witnesses are located in Brooklyn, New York. There is no higher leader than Jehovah, and He works directly through the leaders in this main office. Approximately one hundred branches carry out the directives of the headquarters and represent local congregations. Since the Kingdom is Jehovah's, and He is clearly the source of all authority, the structure is hierarchical, not democratic.

Becoming ordained requires personal dedication to serve Jehovah, made in sincere private prayer through Christ. On doing this, a convert must be baptized in water by immersion, to symbolize complete dedication to Jehovah. Every baptized member is a minister, and this status is commonly used to avoid the military draft.

Each local congregation meets in a Kingdom Hall of Jehovah's Witnesses, but Witnesses believe that buildings themselves are unimportant; the true church is the people of Jehovah. Congregations divide into two groups when membership reaches 200, so most of the buildings are small. Since each member is a minister, Witnesses expect all members to learn to preach and witness. A Theocratic Ministry School meets weekly to train members in the skills of public speaking, Bible memorization, and witnessing. The Sunday meeting consists of a Bible study, which is open to the public, followed by a Watchtower meeting, in which members study the current issues of the magazine, paying particular attention to articles on current events which are fulfillments of biblical prophecy.

Once each year, on the anniversary of Christ's death, members partake of unleavened bread and red wine in a service of communion. Only the most devout partake (according to personal choice) and those who do not partake are still expected to attend.

Jehovah's Witnesses are highly visible in North America because of their organization and aggressiveness, and because of their freedom to advance their beliefs here. In many nations governed by authoritarian hierarchies (ironically, the Witnesses' own form of government), they are not free to use their methods of witnessing. Wherever

Jehovah's Witnesses work, they offend some Christian people.

Many Christians throughout the world will not converse openly with the Witnesses because of their aggressive method. In addition, they know that Jehovah's Witnesses do not represent the truth of God's whole revelation, nor are they open to Christ, nor do they display respect for true evangelism. (True evangelism presents the whole Word of God, is nonmanipulative, and respects the work of the Holy Spirit in the hearts of people.)

As Christians, we support the freedom of Jehovah's Witnesses to practice their methods, because freedom is preferable to an authoritarian culture, and we are confident that God's truth will overcome. But we also retain our freedom to decline to lend an ear to what we know is false.

Questions

1. Evaluating the Jehovah's Witnesses' view of Christ, someone observed, "They believe that Christ *affected* people's salvation, but didn't *effect* it." What did the observer mean? Do you agree?

2. Read the Bible verses which allegedly teach us not to accept blood transfusions or eat foods containing blood (Lev. 3:17; Deut. 12:27). Do you agree or disagree with the Jehovah's Witnesses' interpretation? Why?

3. How do you react to the Witnesses' beliefs about the Christian concept of the Trinity? Can you support your reaction with Scripture?

4. Read Romans 8:34 and Hebrews 4:14–16. In what ways do Jehovah's Witnesses limit their appreciation of Christ by rejecting His bodily resurrection and ascension?

5. Do you think the prediction of the destruction of the present world order is consistent with Jehovah's love? Explain.

6. What do you find in the beliefs of Jehovah's Witnesses that is comforting? Threatening?

Additional Sources of Information

Books

Hoekema, Anthony A. *Jehovah's Witnesses*. Grand Rapids: Eerdmans, 1974.
A scholarly study of the theology of Jehovah's Witnesses from a biblical perspective. This book also appears as a chapter in Hoekema's *The Four Major Cults* (Eerdmans, 1963).

Jehovah's Witnesses in the Twentieth Century. New York: Watchtower Bible and Tract Society of New York, 1979.
A thirty-one-page booklet by the Jehovah's Witnesses, describing how they see themselves.

Martin, Walter, and Klann, Norman H. *Jehovah of the Watchtower*. Chicago: Moody, 1974.
This is a totally revised and updated edition of this book. The first part of the book relates the lives of leaders of the Jehovah's Witnesses and traces the development of the organization. The major part of the book is a comparison between the doctrines of the Witnesses and the Word of God.

Schnell, William J. *Thirty Years a Watchtower Slave*. Grand Rapids: Baker, 1971.
This book is an interesting account of a person who was a member of the Jehovah's Witnesses from the 1920s to the 1940s. It gives insight into the organization and its leaders.

Stevenson, William C. *The Inside Story of Jehovah's Witnesses*. New York: Hart, 1968.
This well-written book is a study of the people, organization, and teachings of Jehovah's Witnesses by a man who was a member in England for fourteen years.

Martin, Walter. "Jehovah's Witnesses, Jesus Christ and the Holy Trinity." Santa Ana, CA: Vision House, 1974.

3

The angel Moroni announces the new gospel for the latter days. A statue of this angel appears atop the Mormon temple in Salt Lake City.

Church of Jesus Christ of Latter-day Saints

Many people know about the Mormons, whose official name is the Church of Jesus Christ of Latter-day Saints. Many people have heard the three-hundred-and-seventy-five-voice choir, accompanied by one of the largest and finest organs in North America. With its weekly broadcast "direct from Temple Square," the Mormon Tabernacle Choir has earned a reputation for quality musical performance, attested by a number of best-selling record albums. From time to time, the *Reader's Digest* carries a paid advertisement explaining the seven keys to Mormonism and reflecting the high ideals of the Mormon faith. The seven keys are "Home and Family Come First," "Try Always to Stand on Your Own Feet," "Work Is Something to Enjoy," "Life Is a Blessing and a Responsibility," "Temperance: for Health and Happiness," "You Learn—That You May Serve," and "Faith Makes You Welcome Each New Day."

The Mormons' positive ideals, combined with

51

a worldwide missionary outreach to which young Mormon men dedicate two years of mission service, have led to phenomenal growth. According to Mormon sources, the church doubled its size between 1965 and 1980. A prestigious national trade journal, *Building Design and Construction*, recently reported that the Mormon church is now the largest private developer in the United States, and that statement does not reflect the church's dramatic worldwide activity. The church has 400–500 chapels and other buildings under construction on any given day, and has about the same number of architects under contract. Two or more congregations share each chapel on a rotating schedule. Although most of its members live in the United States, the Mormon church has a Canadian membership of 89,000. More than half a million Mormons live in Central and South America. The Mormons also have won thousands of converts in Europe, Asia, and the South Pacific. Many of their manuals and instructional materials are published in seventy languages. Teams of translators are now working to expand the number of languages to more than 200. As a direct result of Mormon mission efforts, the membership of the Church of Jesus Christ of Latter-day Saints has passed the five million mark.

Mormon beliefs, which originated with Joseph Smith, have been defined and elaborated by subsequent church presidents whom, along with Smith, the Mormons regard as divine prophets. The first part of this chapter presents the life of Joseph Smith and the origin of Mormon beliefs, including a survey of the *Book of Mormon*. The second part of this chapter includes a summary of modern Mormon beliefs.

The Origin of Mormon Beliefs

The Life of Joseph Smith

Soon after Joseph Smith was born in Vermont in 1805, the Smith family moved to New York State. Most of the family became Presbyterian, but Joseph was confused by the conflicting claims of the churches in the area, all of which claimed to be the one true church. Following the Bible's advice, "If any of you lack wisdom, let him ask of God, that giveth to all men liberally ... and it shall be given him" (James 1:5, KJV), Joseph went into a forest to pray for guidance. Praying aloud for the first time in his life, he withdrew into a spiritual experience which ended when he discovered that he was lying on his back, looking up into the sky. Fifteen years later, recalling what had happened, Joseph Smith wrote:

> ... I saw two Personages, whose brightness and glory defy all description, standing above me in the air. One of them spake unto me, calling me by name and said—pointing to the other—*This is My Beloved Son. Hear Him.*
>
> My object in going to inquire of the Lord was to know which of all the sects was right, that I might know which to join. No sooner, therefore, did I get possession of myself, so as to be able to speak, than I asked the Personages who stood above me in the

light, which of all the sects was right—and which I should join.

I was answered that I must join none of them, for they were all wrong; and the Personage who addressed me said that all their creeds were an abomination in his sight; that those professors were all corrupt; that; "they draw near to me with their lips, but their hearts are far from me; they teach for doctrines the commandments of men, having a form of godliness, but they deny the power thereof."

He again forbade me to join with any of them. . . .[1]

Based on revelation, Latter-day Saints believe that an apostasy arose following the deaths of Jesus and the apostles. Changes were made in the gospel of Jesus Christ, and the authority to act in God's name was lost to humans. Therefore, the personage told Joseph Smith to join none of the "sects," for those who originated their creeds were not authorized to do so.

Such a blatantly negative attitude toward the Christian church is rarely found among Mormons today. Modern Mormons interpret the personage's statement to mean that those religious leaders who made changes in the gospel of Jesus Christ were condemned. There is no condemnation, according to the Mormons, of members who innocently follow these creeds.

What is known about Joseph Smith, the fourteen-year-old boy who claimed to receive new revelations from God? It would be unfair to dis-

1. Joseph Smith, *The Pearl of Great Price* (Salt Lake City: The Church of Jesus Christ of Latter-day Saints), p. 48.

credit Joseph Smith without seeking to understand the historical setting from which he came and the forces that shaped him. On the other hand, it would be irresponsible to accept Smith's claims without studying the circumstances which convinced him that he was a prophet of the latter days. So let's recall the character of New York State in the early nineteenth century and the forces that affected Smith as he grew up.

The Religious Climate

During Joseph Smith's boyhood, turbulence and instability plagued many American churches, including the denominations in New York State. Frustrating economic conditions, frequent uprooting of families, difficult frontier life and the stubborn individualism of the early settlers contributed to religious unrest. Extreme personal misfortune produced excesses of belief and practice, often dividing congregations. The Baptist church, for instance, became these distinct Baptist denominations: Reformed, Hard-Shell, Free-Will, Seventh-Day, and Footwashing Baptists. The Methodist church, also plagued by factionalism, divided into four splinter groups in the years between Joseph's ninth and twenty-fifth birthdays. Each group confidently claimed that it was the pure, restored, primitive Christian Church and that its was the only correct understanding of the Bible.

Palmyra, New York, Joseph's home after age ten, was the center of what later writers described as the "burnt-over district of New York." Traveling preachers, usually uneducated, went from town to town holding frenzied revival meetings. To arouse the people spiritually, preachers commonly terrified backsliders into repentance, stoked the fires of hell for unbelievers, and graphically described the torments awaiting the unrepentant as well as the heavenly delights awaiting the repentant. Frightened, guilt-ridden, repentant sinners crowded forward to makeshift altars to be spiritually reborn. The revival meetings often went out of control as the saved were overcome with emotion. Many shouted their hallelujahs, some spoke in tongues, some made barking noises, some fell to the ground apparently unconscious, and some experienced uncontrollable shaking and jerking. One religious group, the Shakers, regarded uncontrolled shaking a mark of true conversion. They are of special interest to our study, because some Shakers settled near Joseph Smith's boyhood home.

The founder of the Shakers, Ann Lee, called herself the reincarnated Christ and claimed to receive special revelations directly from God. Lee and her celibate followers moved into New York State where eccentric religious tastes allowed them to flourish. By the time Joseph Smith was twenty-one, the Shakers had built places of worship only thirty miles from Palmyra. (In 1831, Smith would claim a revelation that declared the Shakers' teachings false.)

But western New York State provided fertile soil for an even more eccentric person, Jemima Wilkinson. She lived just twenty-four miles from the ten-year-old Smith. Claiming to be a female

Christ, she gathered a colony of followers with whom she shared her steady stream of divine revelations from heaven. Even more bizarre was her assistant, called the Prophet Elijah, who claimed to induce heavenly prophecies by tightly wrapping his waist until his abdomen grew enormously. Finally, he would begin to prophesy profusely, and as he did, his abdomen would deflate to normal size. Elijah confirmed Jemima's divine revelation that she would live forever. When Joseph was twelve, however, Jemima reportedly died, although her followers persistently denied it. It was years before local authorities declared her legally dead and the colony disbanded.

During Joseph's early years, another nonconformist, Isaac Bullard, and his pilgrim followers settled within walking distance of the Smith family farm. Wearing only a bearskin and bragging that he had not changed his clothing for seven years, Bullard advocated a communal life of complete equality, common ownership of property, and free love. Although communes have become well-known in recent years, it may come as some surprise to learn that scores of them existed during the time of Joseph Smith.

Joseph Smith, a man of many noble qualities, grew up in troubled times. It is impossible to say how much the eccentric people around him influenced him. But the turbulent religious climate does explain the readiness of many people to follow radical new ideas. And when Joseph Smith supplied an answer to a question prevalent during his boyhood—Where did the American Indian come from?—many were ready to hear his most famous revelation.

The Native-American Mystery

What captured the attention of young Joseph Smith were the *tumuli*, or ancient burial mounds, near his home. There was considerable speculation about who were buried in the tumuli and how they got there. Many people believed that an ancient civilization had been extinguished, and the final victims of the war had been buried in the tumuli. When Joseph was thirteen, the local newspaper carried a story advancing the theory that Native Americans had been buried in the tumuli, but critics replied that the pottery and copper found in the tumuli were of much higher quality than that of the Native Americans. Another theory in circulation at this time claimed that the people buried in the tumuli had been a peaceful community of farmers and metalworkers who were slain by a savage race of people related to the contemporary Native American.

A theory circulated among frontier ministers shed light on unanswered questions of the Bible. Jonathan Edwards, among others, advanced the belief that the lost tribes of Israel were buried in the tumuli. The resemblance between Native American and Hebrew languages led Edwards to believe it possible that Old Testament Jews had migrated to America and formed communities, but had later been wiped out, leaving behind the tumuli. Edwards's theory was the most popular explanation while Joseph Smith was growing up.

Historical documents indicate that Joseph spent many boyhood days digging and exploring among these mounds. At least eight tumuli were located within twelve miles of his home. Joseph also engaged in the practice of gazing into a peep-stone to locate hidden treasures in the earth. Money digging is not to Joseph's discredit, since locating ancient treasures was an ingrained part of rural folklore. Young Joseph, along with his father and neighbors, unearthed many ancient artifacts, including pottery, copper decorations, jewelry, ancient breastplates—even ornaments in the shape of the cross!

Joseph found these discoveries very exciting. According to his mother, he had long been absorbed in theories about the tumuli:

> During our evening conversations, Joseph would occasionally give us some of the most amusing recitals that could be imagined. He would describe the ancient inhabitants of this continent, their dress, mode of traveling, and the animals on which they rode; their cities, their buildings, with every particular; their mode of warfare; and also their religious worship. This he would do with as much ease, seemingly, as if he had spent his whole life with them.[2]

Joseph's fascination with the ancient inhabitants of this continent led to his best-known revelation, the *Book of Mormon*. Before examining that reve-

2. Fawn M. Brodie, *No Man Knows My History: The Life of Joseph Smith, the Mormon Prophet*, second edition, revised and enlarged (New York: Alfred A. Knopf, 1957), p. 35.

lation, however, we will briefly consider his family background.

The unsettled religious climate in New York affected Joseph's family. His grandfather on his mother's side was a nonconformist who believed that each person should rely on individual religious experience. Joseph's Uncle Jason followed this advice and became a Seeker, a member of a Christian commune of thirty families. Hampered by lack of education and lifelong poverty, Joseph's father taught him rural folklore, including money digging, water witching, and the use of peepstones to locate hidden treasures in the earth. Although Joseph's mother was a devoutly religious person, given to mysticism, her religious allegiances never resulted in active church membership, because the bickering and self-righteous claims of various churches left her confused. Young Joseph once had a religious experience at a Methodist camp meeting; in fact, he became a fairly good exhorter at some of these meetings, but he despised the sectarian self-righteousness of the churches. As far as he was concerned, no single church knew more about the Kingdom of God than did any other. His early vision, at age fourteen, may have been precipitated by his family's reaction to the established church. We know his first vision resolved his nagging concern about which church to join; now we will note how the instability of the times became even more apparent in another vision about three years later.

Moroni's Visit

Just two months before his eighteenth birthday, Joseph recalled, he was kneeling by his bed to seek forgiveness for his sins. Suddenly his room was flooded with light and a personage appeared in the air. He was magnificent, and was dressed in a long, loose white robe. The visitor, whose name was Moroni, was the son of Mormon, a prophet who had lived in North America. He addressed Joseph by name and told him that God had a special task for him to do. He warned Joseph that people would speak both good and evil of him in all nations. He told Joseph of a book, written by Mormon on golden plates, which had been buried with two stones, the Urim and Thummim, which God had supplied for translating the book. Moroni told Joseph that the book contained the story of the previous inhabitants of North America and gave account of their origins. According to Joseph, Moroni said that the plates contained the true gospel, which had been delivered by the Savior to the previous inhabitants of North America.

For some reason, Joseph was reluctant to speak publicly about the appearance of Moroni. When begged by a church council many years later, Joseph declined to tell the story because it was simply not advisable for him to speak about it. The full details were released fifteen years later, when the church was established and Smith wrote his official history. The plates, he recalled, were uncovered in a stone box along with the Old Testament stones, the Urim and Thummim (cf. Exod. 28:30; Num. 27:21). However, he was forbidden to touch the plates until he was adequately purified and prepared. Once a year Joseph returned to the spot, Hill Cumorah, near Palmyra, New York, and on the fourth year, when Joseph was twenty-one, he was permitted to remove the plates for translation.

What is known of Joseph's life during this four-year period hardly suggests that he lived in awe of the heavenly visitor. Court records reveal that Smith was tried for being a disorderly person and an imposter. Sworn testimony describes Joseph's money digging activities with the aid of a magic stone at age twenty. About fifteen years later, P. Hurlbut, a one-time Mormon excommunicated for immoral conduct, collected sworn statements from dozens of Joseph's friends, acquaintances, and neighbors to discredit his discovery of the *Book of Mormon*. One might well question the motives of Hurlbut in collecting these legal affidavits, as well as the motives of those who supplied them, but the fact that people produced signed statements, exposing themselves to legal liability, increases the value and authenticity of these reports. Perhaps Smith's behavior can be explained, but it can hardly be denied. Despite his questionable activities, the twenty-one-year-old prophet claimed the golden plates, and the *Book of Mormon* resulted.

The Book of Mormon

Translation of the characters on the golden plates continued for three years, in spurts of prolific activity. Smith translated the information inscribed in an unknown language called Reformed Egyptian, sometimes by peering at the Old Testament stones and sometimes by looking into the bottom of his hat, unaided by the Urim and Thummim. As he dictated, a secretary on the opposite side of the room wrote down the deciphered text, word for word. Since no one was permitted to examine the plates or to observe Joseph while he translated (by threat of death by divine wrath), a blanket was hung between Smith and the translator. Within three years, the translation was complete.

Although the plates were never examined, several witnesses testified that they had seen them. Some later retracted their testimony and left the church, but others told how they had seen the plates with "eyes of faith." Shortly afterward, according to Joseph Smith, an angel messenger removed the plates to heaven. However, Smith did copy some of the letters from the golden plates for a prospective investor. The letters bear no resemblance to Egyptian, and Professor Charles Anthon of New York City, whom Mormons claim verified the letters, subsequently wrote an angry disclaimer calling the event a hoax designed to bilk the investor of his money. Figure 1 shows the letters said to have been copied from the golden plates.

In the spring of 1980, a Mormon historian uncovered the original characters (letters) taken to Anthon. On the page, in Joseph Smith's handwriting, was this message: "These caractors were dilligently coppied by my own hand from the plates of gold and given to Martin Harris, who took them to New York Citty, but the learned could not translate it because the Lord would not open it to them in fulfillment of the prophecy of Isaih

63

Figure 1*

*As reproduced in Fawn M. Brodie's *No Man Knows My History: The Life of Joseph Smith, the Mormon Prophet* (New York: Alfred A. Knopf, 1957), facing p. 51.

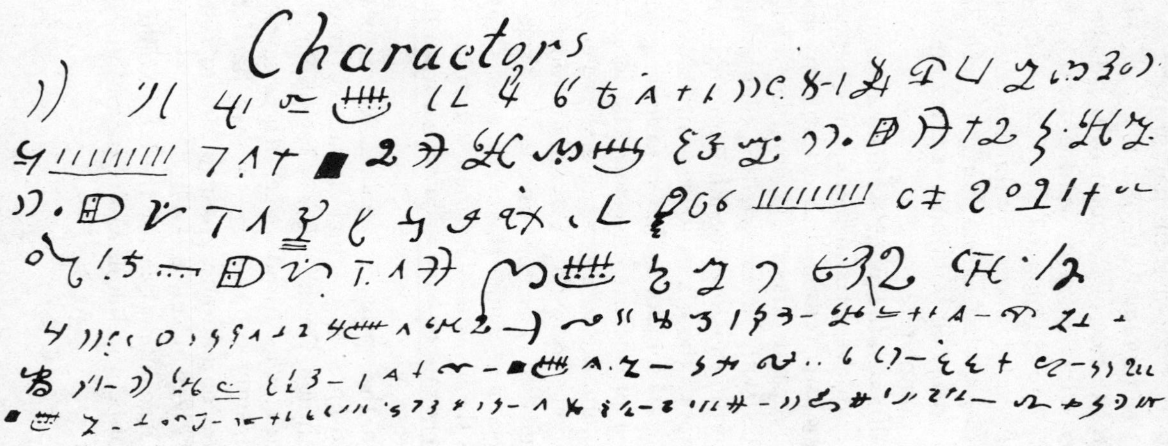

Characters

written in the 29th chapter and 11th verse. Joseph Smith, Jr."[3]

The completed translation of the *Book of Mormon* resolved the question of the Native Americans' origin. The main characters of the *Book of Mormon* are Nephi and Laman, two Jewish brothers who, with four other brothers, emigrated to the Americas from Jerusalem around 600 B.C. They were directed by God to sail across the ocean with their families and possessions in a barge made according to divine instruction. The brothers, from oldest to youngest, were Laman, Lemuel, Nephi, Sam, Jacob, and Joseph. The two oldest brothers were evil, belligerent young men who disobeyed God. Because they constantly harassed Nephi and the younger, pious, obedient brothers, God pronounced judgment on them: He cursed Laman and Lemuel with dark skin. Meanwhile Nephi and his three younger brothers lived obedient lives. They reared families of white children. Two races, the Nephites and the Lamanites, grew up in South and North America, spreading across the continents from sea to sea.

Because of their faithful obedience to God, the Nephites were rewarded with a personal visit from the resurrected and ascended Christ. Appearing to the Nephites at Temple Bountiful, Jesus announced His victorious death and preached a series of sermons (*Book of Mormon*, III Nephi 11–29). This appearance of Christ in North America explained why crosses were sometimes uncovered in the burial mounds.

3. *Deseret News*, Monday, April 28, 1980, p. 1.

After many cycles of war and peace, burial mounds dotted the countryside. Each mound contained the remains of war victims. Eventually the Nephites were destroyed, but not before a staunch Nephite by the name of Mormon had documented their history in Reformed Egyptian (*Book of Mormon*, Mormon 9:32–33). Buried in A.D. 421, this document remained buried near Palmyra until 1827, when Moroni directed Smith to its exact location. The Lamanites remained, as savage, bloodthirsty people, scattered throughout the Americas. Clearly, the mysteries of the burial mounds and the Native Americans' origin were solved by the history contained in the *Book of Mormon*.

Although Mormons claim archaeological proof for the *Book of Mormon* (largely dependent on remains of Aztec civilization and the legendary visit of a great white god), no proof exists for most of the details in the *Book of Mormon*. Several implausible passages have brought considerable doubt and criticism. One passage, for example, describes how ancient inhabitants brought to the Americas oxen, cows, sheep, swine, goats, horses, asses, elephants, curelom, and cremoms (*Book of Mormon*, Ether 9:18–19). The identity of the last two is unknown, the presence of elephants defies credibility, and the transport of swine by Jews seems unlikely. Passages such as this have caused many people to view the *Book of Mormon* as little more than a record of Joseph Smith's fantasies. A famous contemporary of Smith's called it "chloroform in print."

Not only the history but also the contents of

the *Book of Mormon* raise questions. A careful study of the *Book of Mormon* reveals that large sections were taken from the King James Version of the Bible. In a book approximately the size of the New Testament, some 27,000 words (25,000 from the Old Testament and 2,000 from the New Testament) appear in the *Book of Mormon* exactly as they appear in the King James Version. Also, the *Book of Mormon* claims that Jesus was born in Jerusalem and introduces John the Baptist, preaching in the village of Bethbara. According to the *Book of Mormon*, the Nephites produced wheat and barley, not the corn and potatoes native to America. The Mormons have developed explanations for every inconsistency within the *Book of Mormon*. Furthermore, the book itself covers the possibility of being discredited due to errors, when Moroni explains that if it could have been written in Hebrew, there would have been no imperfection in the record (Moroni 9:33).

When Smith published the *Book of Mormon* and claimed that it was a divine revelation, he became the victim of sarcastic mockery. But some people believed and developed a fanatic loyalty to Joseph Smith. Soon the Church of Jesus Christ of Latter-day Saints was established. Joseph Smith went on to become a prophet in demand, general of the Mormon army, husband of four dozen wives, and presidential candidate. What transpired in the mind of Joseph Smith during these years remains an open question. A few months before his death, Smith told a huge audience, "You don't know me; you never knew my heart. No man knows my history. I cannot tell it; I shall never undertake it. I don't blame anyone for not believing my history. If I had not experienced what I have, I could not have believed it myself."[4]

The Effect of Smith's Revelations and Death

Joseph Smith, encouraged by the early acceptance of his teaching and the growing loyalty of believers, began to claim an increasing number and variety of revelations. These are included in two other scriptures: *Doctrine and Covenants* and *Pearl of Great Price*. These later revelations, more than the *Book of Mormon*, became the sources of enduring doctrines of Mormonism.

Smith's revelations ranged from the significant to the trivial. One revelation claimed that Negroes were cursed by God with black skin, and must submit to God-ordained servitude, a revelation which was replaced by a new one in 1978. When his followers began using peepstones, Smith forbade the practice by claiming a divine revelation. He also claimed a revelation that Native Americans would turn white following conversion to the restored gospel. His adoring followers gladly accepted the revelation that the Garden of Eden was located just outside of Independence, Missouri. Many of his revelations, however, covered trivial events and daily routines.

Some of Smith's revelations to his followers

4. Brodie, *No Man Knows My History*, p. vii.

were not fulfilled. This gave them occasion to apply the biblical test of prophecy: "If what a prophet proclaims in the name of the Lord does not take place or come true, that is a message the Lord has not spoken . . ." (Deut. 18:22). Many took this test seriously and as a result, Smith left disillusioned, angry, and broken ex-followers who never forgave him. Others faithfully followed Smith and welcomed his new revelations, some of which proved very significant for Mormon theology.

Many basic tenets of modern Mormonism resulted directly from Smith's revelations, which revealed to him that God is a physical being, that men can become gods, that there are many gods, that polygamy is God-intended, that there are three distinct heavens, that all people exist in a pre-earth life, and that Jesus is a spirit-child of God. While Smith's followers enthusiastically received new revelations, non-Mormons grew angry and tried to expose Smith as an imposter.

Certain of Smith's revelations, particularly messages about polygamy and secret temple rites, perturbed non-Mormon citizens. Their dislike for Smith grew to overt hostility, spawned by the immorality and secrecy of plural marriages. A local newspaper, the *Nauvoo* (Ill.) *Expositor*, attacked the practice of polygamy and leveled charges of financial and political abuse. Angered by these charges, Smith denounced the newspaper, whereupon a group of Mormons marched to the office, wrecked the printing press, and burned every newspaper they could find.

Following this attack, Joseph Smith was jailed,

with other Mormon leaders, in Carthage, Illinois. An angry mob stormed the jail on June 27, 1844, and shot Smith and his brother. Before his fortieth birthday, the prophet lay dead on a Carthage street. Although Fawn M. Brodie, a Smith biographer, reported that Joseph used a gun that had been smuggled into the jail to fire six times at his attackers, the Mormons have always considered Smith a martyr.

Smith's death left his followers in disarray. His son, Joseph Smith III, claimed his father had blessed and designated him to be the next prophet. Those who followed Joseph's son have become known as the Reorganized Church of Jesus Christ of Latter-day Saints. The group is much smaller than the Mormons, and although its president is a biological descendant of Smith, the Reorganized Church rejects many of Joseph Smith's revelations, such as polygamy and baptism for the dead. James Strang started another faction on Beaver Island in northern Lake Michigan, and established himself as a king, ruling his colony by divine revelation. Another Smith follower went to Texas, another to St. Louis, another to Pittsburgh. All claimed to possess the gifts of divine revelation and prophecy. The most famous follower, Brigham Young, accepted presidency of the apostles and assumed leadership of the Mormon community.

To escape continuing persecution, Brigham Young led the Mormon community to Salt Lake City, Utah. Thousands of Mormons undertook the strenuous journey. Many died enroute, but the survivors finally arrived in the Salt Lake Valley in 1847. For thirty years, Brigham Young consolidated the Mormon people financially, socially, and religiously. Aided by divine revelations, he defined and refined many of Joseph Smith's teachings. Within the community of self-reliant pioneers, Brigham Young established the thriving town of Salt Lake City, where their descendants honor the pioneers each year with a special holiday, July 24, Pioneers' Day.

Mormon Beliefs

The basic beliefs of the Mormon church are contained in thirteen articles of faith written by Joseph Smith. Although these statements appear, on the surface, quite similar to those of the evangelical Christian church, closer examination of Mormon doctrines will reveal considerable differences.

1. We believe in God, the Eternal Father, and in His Son, Jesus Christ, and in the Holy Ghost.
2. We believe that men will be punished for their own sins, and not for Adam's transgression.
3. We believe that through the Atonement of Christ, all mankind may be saved, by obedience to the laws and ordinances of the Gospel.
4. We believe that the first principles and ordinances of the Gospel are: first, Faith in the Lord Jesus Christ; second, Repentance; third, Baptism by immersion for the remission of sins; fourth, Laying on of hands for the gift of the Holy Ghost.

5. We believe that a man must be called of God, by prophecy, and by the laying on of hands, by those who are in authority, to preach the Gospel and administer in the ordinances thereof.

6. We believe in the same organization that existed in the Primitive Church, namely, apostles, prophets, pastors, teachers, evangelists, etc.

7. We believe in the gift of tongues, prophecy, revelation, visions, healing, interpretation of tongues, etc.

8. We believe the Bible to be the word of God as far as it is translated correctly; we also believe the Book of Mormon to be the word of God.

9. We believe all that God has revealed, all that He does now reveal, and we believe that He will yet reveal many great and important things pertaining to the Kingdom of God.

10. We believe in the literal gathering of Israel and in the restoration of the Ten Tribes; that Zion (the New Jerusalem) will be built upon the American continent; that Christ will reign personally upon the earth; and, that the earth will be renewed and receive its paradisiacal glory.

11. We claim the privilege of worshiping Almighty God according to the dictates of our own conscience, and allow all men the same privilege, let them worship how, where, or what they may.

12. We believe in being subject to kings, presi-

dents, rulers, and magistrates, in obeying, honoring, and sustaining the law.

13. We believe in being honest, true, chaste, benevolent, virtuous, and in doing good to all men; indeed, we may say that we follow the admonition of Paul—We believe all things, we hope all things, we have endured many things, and hope to be able to endure all things. If there is anything virtuous, lovely, or of good report or praiseworthy, we seek after these things.

The Nature of God

It has been said that people are known by the hymns they sing. If this is true, then Mormon hymns should teach us something about Mormon beliefs regarding the nature of God. Look for answers to the following five questions in particular as you review these hymns: Where were we before we were born? Who is a spirit-child of God? Is God married? Is there more than one God? Can we become like God?

O My Father

O my Father, Thou that dwellest
In the high and glorious place!
When shall I regain Thy presence
And again behold Thy face?
In Thy holy habitation
Did my spirit once reside,
In my first primeval childhood,
Was I nurtured near Thy side?

For a wise and glorious purpose
Thou hast placed me here on earth,
And withheld the recollection
Of my former friends and birth,
Yet oft-times a secret something
Whispered, 'You're a stranger here';
And I felt that I had wandered
From a more exalted sphere.

I had learned to call Thee Father
Thro' Thy Spirit from on high;
But until the Key of Knowledge
Was restored, I knew not why.
In the heavens are parents single?
No; the tho't makes reason stare!
Truth is reason, truth eternal
Tells me I've a mother there.

When I leave this frail existence,
When I lay this mortal by,
Father, Mother, may I meet you
In your royal courts on high?
Then, at length, when I've completed
All you sent me forth to do.
With your mutual approbation
Let me come and dwell with you.[5]

If You Could Hie to Kolob

If you could hie to Kolob,
In th' twinkling of an eye,
And then continue onward,
With that same speed to fly,
D'ye think that you could ever,
Through all eternity,
Find out the generation
Where Gods began to be?

5. *Hymns* (Salt Lake City, UT: Deseret Book Co.), no. 139.

The works of God continue,
And worlds and lives abound;
Improvement and progression
Have one eternal round.
There is no end to matter,
There is no end to space,
There is no end to spirit,
There is no end to race.[6]

These hymns give us the basics, but we need more information to understand the Mormon view of God's nature. Placed in sequence, here are some Mormon teachings.

1. Before the earth was created, a council of gods decided to organize and populate the planet Earth.
2. A god who was exalted on the planet Kolob came to earth with his celestial wife. Given physical bodies, they became Adam and Eve. After Eve's sin, Adam transgressed the law and became mortal in order to propagate the earth. (Transgression is *willing* but not *willful* disobedience.)
3. God was once as we are—human. By a series of progressions or exaltations, he became God. Hence the famous Mormon couplet, "As man is now, God once was; As God is now, man may become."
4. All human beings existed in eternity—in a preearth life—as spirit-children of God. The first spirit-child was Christ, our "eldest brother" and the "first begotten son of God."

6. *Ibid.*, no. 257.

5. God places us on earth and gives us bodies as a probation to test us. He withdraws from us any memory of our pre-earth life.
6. If we successfully obey gospel ordinances and prove ourselves during our earthly probation, we can progress and advance to higher levels. Eventually, we may progress to the exalted position of a god, and populate another planet in limitless space.
7. God has a body of flesh and bone, as tangible as the one you have now.
8. Only by obedience and repentance can we become one with the gods, but this can be achieved by any person in our probationary state.

This framework clearly shows that Mormons believe that God has a body of flesh and bone, that He is an exalted man, that He is one of many gods existing in many worlds, and that the one God of earth's people is known as the heavenly Father. He created all of our spirits long ago, and these spirits existed with God until they were placed in bodies on earth. Smith once declared,

> The doctrine of a plurality of Gods is as prominent in the Bible as any other doctrine. It is all over the face of the Bible. It stands beyond the power of controversy. . . . The heads of the gods appointed one God for us; and when you take that view of the subject, it sets one free to see the beauty, holiness and perfection of the gods.[7]

7. Joseph Fielding Smith, ed., *Teaching of the Prophet Joseph Smith* (Salt Lake City, UT: Deseret Book Co., 1958), pp. 370, 372.

With regard to the Trinity, Mormons speak of the Holy Spirit as a divine energy of God, an impersonal spiritual force or "personage of spirit" which is given to God's children during their earthly probation. Jesus' unity with God is a unity of will, not a unity of person. In Mormon theology, Jesus' claim that He and His Father are one (John 17:22) means that Jesus and the Father are united in purpose, nothing more. Fortified by his first vision, Smith insisted that God and Christ appeared to him as "distinct personages" which, he taught, meant they were neither equal nor united. But let's examine more closely the Mormon teaching about Jesus.

Teachings about Christ

The person of Christ. We noted earlier that Mormons view Jesus as the first spirit-child created by God. After His creation, others came into existence and looked to Jesus as their elder brother. We did not mention at that time the Mormon belief that Jehovah actually was Christ in His pre-earth life. Mormons distinguish Elohim (our Father) from Jehovah (pre-incarnate Christ). As Jehovah, Christ created the world under the direction of the heavenly Father. Yet, no less than any other person who ever lived, Jesus was a spirit-child of God (Elohim). Obviously then, Mormons believe Jesus is divine but do not believe that he was God incarnate.

Two features of Mormon ideas about Jesus are outstanding. First, some Mormons have taught that Jesus practiced polygamy, that He was the husband of Mary, Martha, and another Mary at the wedding in Cana of Galilee. Second, some Mormon prophets have claimed that Jesus was conceived when God the Father and the virgin Mary had intercourse, although the church has not officially accepted this theory. Mormons consider Christ unique because He is the oldest and firstborn, the offspring of a mortal mother and immortal Father, selected by the Father to be Redeemer and Savior, and because He was sinless. Christians consider Jesus Christ *Immanuel*, God with us; Mormons consider Jesus Christ the older brother, the firstborn child of God.

The role of Christ. To understand the Mormon view of Christ's role in salvation, we must understand the meaning of the third article of faith, which states, "We believe that through the Atonement of Christ, all mankind may be saved, by obedience to the laws and ordinances of the Gospel." What is this salvation? Mormons use the term *general salvation*, which is a synonym for resurrection from the dead. Christ, by His death, has assured that all people will be resurrected, no matter what their conduct has been. In this sense, Mormons believe that everyone will be saved (resurrected), but not all will earn the rewards of the celestial and terrestrial kingdoms (heavens). Here we must proceed thoughtfully, for we will discover that Mormons believe a person can be saved (resurrected) because of Christ's atonement, but not go to heaven. From this distinction comes the warning familiar to young Mormons: "salvation without exaltation is damnation." A study of the

Mormon understanding of salvation shows how a person can be saved from death through the resurrection, but not be saved into the presence of the eternal Father.

Another facet of redemption for Mormons is *exaltation*. By exaltation, Mormons mean the entrance into one of three heavenly kingdoms. Obedience to the gospel ordinances and acceptance of the restored gospel of Mormonism alone gain a person exaltation in the world to come. In other words, Christ's death gives us immortality (victory over physical death), but whether we are exalted depends on the way we live during our time of earthly probation. In this sense, a person can gain salvation (immortality), but fail to achieve exaltation (life in heaven). Quite obviously, the importance of Christ in the plan of salvation is lessened by these beliefs. Mormons cannot say that Jesus died for our salvation to eternal life in heaven, only that Jesus died to make it possible for us to *achieve* exaltation. This of course introduces salvation through works, but before reviewing this idea, let's seek to understand the broader scope of salvation in Mormon theology by referring to Figure 2.

During the pre-earth spirit life in heaven, a revolt resulted in some spirits being cast into the realm of Satan. These spirits also come to earth to live within people. This accounts for cases of demonic possession.

The arrows in Figure 2 indicate that there are four destinies for human beings. The first, reserved for those who obediently follow the Mormon faith and gospel ordinances, is paradise, a pleasant

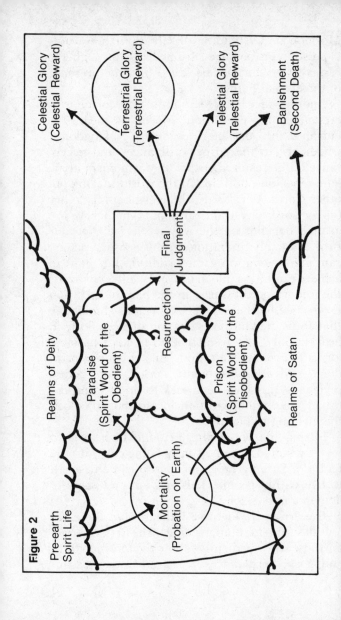

Figure 2

Pre-earth Spirit Life

Mortality (Probation on Earth)

Realms of Deity

Paradise (Spirit World of the Obedient)

Resurrection

Prison (Spirit World of the Disobedient)

Realms of Satan

Final Judgment

Celestial Glory (Celestial Reward)

Terrestrial Glory (Terrestrial Reward)

Telestial Glory (Telestial Reward)

Banishment (Second Death)

place for education and progression. The second destiny is reserved for those of Christian denominations, those who have never learned of Mormonism, and Mormons who have demonstrated inadequate obedience. People in these categories go to a prison to be taught the gospel, with the option of accepting it. As we will see later, Mormons practice baptism for the dead, a practice which they claim assures us that dead ancestors who are in prison will have opportunity to accept the gospel. The disobedient remain in prison until the final judgment.

At the final judgment, all residents of paradise and prison will be resurrected. The most devout Mormons will enter the highest reward, which is called celestial glory. The less devout Mormons and most devout Christians will enter terrestrial glory. Those who are worthy of immortality, but not much else, will enter the lowest heaven, telestial glory.

The Way of Salvation

So much of this chapter has stressed the value of works in salvation that it seems redundant to discuss it further. Yet two brief distinctions must be made.

Mormonism stresses the absolute necessity of good works to achieve exaltation. Mormons often present their views with an agreeable emphasis on faith in Christ, but this refers to Christ's gift of immortality, not exaltation. Exaltation, in Mormon teaching and practice, is related to the accumulation of good works.

Mormonism stresses the absolute necessity of good works to determine which of the three heavenly kingdoms a believer will enter. The sole criterion to determine a believer's level of exaltation will be the level of that person's obedience to the Mormon faith and scriptural ordinances.

The Bible

Mormons believe that the Bible is God's infallible Word, and even include the following statement of faith in *Pearl of Great Price*: "We believe the Bible to be the Word of God. . . ." However, three facts render this statement of faith meaningless.

The Bible is accepted as God's message to the old world, presumably the world of the Middle East and of time long past. In fact, Mormons do not believe that the Bible is God's final Word, nor His best Word, nor His Word for our continent in these "latter days." For the Mormons, the Bible contains information that is obsolete.

The Bible is accepted "insofar as it is translated correctly." Mormon missionaries stoutly claim that many errors crept into the Bible while many "plain and precious truths were removed." As a result, Bible truths had to be restored, which is why Joseph Smith was given a new revelation, a restoration of the plain and precious truths.

Mormons rely far more on divine revelation outside of the Bible than they do on the Bible. In fact, their other scriptures and the continuing revelations through the First Presidency of the Church are never tested against biblical revelation; they are merely imposed on the Bible. Therefore, the Bible is treated as an obsolete and incomplete revelation which can be properly understood only in the light of newer revelations made through Joseph Smith the prophet, and the line of prophets since his time.

The Organization of the Mormon Church

The Restored Church

Mormons believe that their church organization, as much as their doctrine, is a direct result of divine revelation. Just like the church of biblical times, the Mormons explain, the modern church must have three essential components: the priesthood, apostles, and prophets. After the death of the original twelve apostles, the offices of priest and prophet dissolved, divine revelation ceased, and the church lost its authority and validity. Beginning with Joseph Smith, the true church with divine authority and organization was restored. Figure 3 illustrates the restored offices.

Both the Aaronic and Melchizedek priesthoods, restored to Joseph Smith through divine revelation, occupy a central place in Mormon church life. Every Mormon male is ordained at age twelve into the lesser priesthood, the Aaronic (Exod. 28:1; 29:1–46; 30:30), and receives the title of deacon. At age fourteen, if he proves worthy, he can become a teacher within the Aaronic priesthood, and at age sixteen he can become a priest. Only

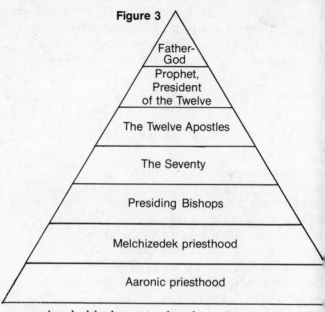

Figure 3

Father-God

Prophet, President of the Twelve

The Twelve Apostles

The Seventy

Presiding Bishops

Melchizedek priesthood

Aaronic priesthood

males hold the priesthood, and prior to 1978 blacks were barred from the office.

At age nineteen, members of the Aaronic priesthood may be ordained into the higher office, the Melchizedek priesthood (Heb. 5:4–10). All Mormon missionaries must attain this office before serving; all Mormon young men who attain the high-priesthood are called *elders*.

An extension of the Melchizedek priesthood is a group called The Seventy. Several hundred quorums of seventy exist in the church. Their special calling is to perform missionary service under the supervision of the Twelve Apostles.

As Christ called twelve disciples or apostles

(Matt. 10:1–5), the Mormon church is also ruled by The Twelve, each of whom is assigned a geographical area for which he is responsible. This Council of the Twelve possesses the same authority given to the biblical apostles, but only the prophet, who also serves as president of the apostles, together with his two counselors, has all authority. The prophet, who is considered a fulfillment of biblical prophecy (Deut. 18:18), rules the church and acts as recipient of divine revelations. To maintain communication in this hierarchy, Mormons from around the world gather in Salt Lake City twice every year to attend general conferences. Attending the conference is a highlight in the lives of individual Mormons, because here they receive direction and guidance from the prophet, the twelve apostles, and other authorities.

Mormons claim to be the one true church, because they alone, of all denominations and churches, have a prophet, twelve apostles, the priesthood, and other offices of the New Testament church.

Mormon Practices

The Ordinances

Baptism and communion. Mormons believe that children cannot sin before the age of eight, because they lack a mature understanding of right and wrong. Since baptism remits sins, there is no need for it until a child is eight years old, at which time baptism is done by immersion. To have authority to baptize another person, a Mormon male must be at least a priest of the Aaronic priesthood. At the time of baptism, there is also a laying on of hands, at which time the baptized person receives the Holy Spirit and comes into a close relationship to the heavenly Father. Only one who is an elder or high priest in the Melchizedek priesthood may perform the laying on of hands. Communion is taken with bread and water, both of which represent Christ's body and blood. Any baptized Mormon is allowed to partake of communion.

Baptism for the dead. Mormons believe that entry into God's Kingdom requires baptism. This belief raises questions about what happens to those who have died without being baptized. After all, many people who lived during the time when "the gospel was removed from the earth" had no opportunity to be baptized. These dead, as we observed earlier, now exist in spirit prison, awaiting resurrection at the return of Christ.

Citing I Corinthians 15:29, Mormons practice baptism for the dead. Active, devout Mormons, according to this rite, can be baptized on behalf of those who, unable to be baptized, went to the spirit world's prison after death. Mormons maintain extensive genealogical records in order to help them discover the names of ancestors for whom they can be baptized. Once a name has been discovered, a Mormon can go to the temple and be baptized in the name of the deceased ancestor. That dead relative will then receive opportunity in the spirit world to accept or reject the restored gospel.

Marriage. The Mormon church practices two types of marriage, one for time and the other for eternity. To be married for time, a couple simply repeats their vows in a marriage ceremony conducted by authorized church leaders. This service is similar to marriage ceremonies in Protestant churches and remains in effect until death.

A second type of marriage, sometimes called celestial marriage, is available to Mormons who are deemed especially worthy and devout. Celestial marriages may be solemnized only in a Mormon temple, under the direct authority of the president of the church. Mormons believe that once they are married in the temple, they are married for eternity, provided they live righteous lives. Referring to Matthew 22:30, Mormons claim that celestial marriage must be performed before the resurrection for any person. This is true of those who have died without an opportunity to receive the seal of celestial marriage in this life. Such couples will be able to propagate in the celestial heaven and have mortal children. Marriage for eternity is a highly significant event in the life of a Mormon couple.

Mormon Lifestyle

Mormons are better known for their practices and their disciplined lifestyle than for their doctrinal beliefs. Mormons are counseled against drinking coffee, tea, or alcoholic beverages, or using tobacco. Cola drinks are also frowned on.

Birth control is discouraged, and large families are desirable. One night each week is designated as family night; television is usually turned off as the family spends the entire evening playing games and listening to a gospel talk by the father. Mormons strongly disapprove of the Equal Rights Amendment to the United States Constitution. Mormon families are encouraged to keep a year's supply of food in storage so that they will be prepared for catastrophe. Because Mormons care for fellow believers, a Mormon rarely needs welfare. Their practice of giving at least ten percent of all personal income has made the church flourish financially. Some Mormons also wear special undergarments which remind them of their supreme loyalty to God's commandments, a practice which originated early in the history of the church and is still encouraged. But these examples of Mormon lifestyle are of little significance compared with the radical difference between Mormon teachings and those of historic Christianity. The difference was perhaps best expressed by an early Mormon, Orson Pratt, who clearly saw the profound importance of the new revelations of Mormonism.

> This book [*Book of Mormon*] must either be true or false. . . . If false, it is one of the most cunning, wicked, bold, deep-laid impositions ever palmed upon the world, calculated to deceive and ruin millions who would sincerely receive it as the Word of God, and will suppose themselves securely built upon the rock of truth until they are plunged with their families into hopeless despair.

The nature of the message in the Book of Mormon is such, that if true, no one can possibly be saved and reject it; if false, no one can possibly be saved and receive it. Therefore, every soul in all the world is equally interested in ascertaining its truth or falsity. In a matter of such infinite importance no person should rest satisfied with the conjectures or opinions of others: he should use every exertion himself to become acquainted with the nature of the message: he should carefully examine the evidences on which it is offered to the world: he should, with all patience and perserverance, seek to acquire a certain knowledge as to whether it be of God or not. Without such an investigation in the most careful, candid, and impartial manner, he cannot safely judge without greatly hazarding his future and eternal welfare.[8]

Questions

1. The *Book of Mormon* allegedly explains the origin of the Native North American. According to most non-Mormon historians, how did the Native Americans originate?
2. Study John 1:1–3, Philippians 2:6–8, and John 4:24, using a commentary. What do these passages teach about the deity of Christ and the person of God?
3. According to I John 4:1–3, how must the Christian discern the "spirit of the antichrist"?
4. Read about the Aztec legend of a great white god. How does this compare with the alleged visit of Jesus to this continent, as described in the *Book of Mormon*?
5. What action has the Mormon church taken to oppose

8. Arthur Budvarson, *The Book of Mormon Examined* (Salt Lake City, UT: Christian Tract Society, 1959)

the Equal Rights Amendment in the United States? Why?

6. In *A New American History*, W. E. Woodword claims,

> In mental and moral make-up he [Brigham Young] was a sort of combination of the outstanding qualities of Jay Gould, Andrew Carnegie and Al Capone, with more than a dash of the oily sanctity of a camp-meeting revivalist. He was too shrewd to be a religious fanatic, and was probably a lifelong hypocrite without any belief whatever in Joseph Smith's fantastic revelations. But he knew the value of a collective fervor in controlling and directing masses of people.[9]

Locate a few references to Brigham Young in books of American history and compare these with Woodword's opinion.

7. Locate an example of Egyptian hieroglyphic writing like that deciphered by Champollion in 1822. How does this compare with the characters allegedly copied from the golden plates?

8. How would you respond to a Mormon who says, "Our church has a clear line of authority to God. What is the basis of your church's authority?"

9. Some claim that II Corinthians 11:14 helps to explain the origin of Mormonism. Do you agree or disagree? Why?

9. (New York: The Literary Guild, 1937), p. 424.

Additional Sources of Information

Books

Anderson, Einar. *Inside Story of Mormonism*. Grand Rapids: Kregel, 1974.
Anderson, a former Mormon who is now a Christian evangelist, gives insight into Mormonism, its history, and its teachings.

Hoekema, Anthony A. *Mormonism*. Grand Rapids: Eerdmans, 1974.
A scholarly study of the theology of Mormonism from a biblical perspective. This is also a chapter in his book, *The Four Major Cults* (Eerdmans, 1963).

Martin, Walter. *The Maze of Mormonism*. Santa Ana, CA: Vision House, revised edition, 1979.
A thoroughly documented historial and theological survey of Mormonism by an evangelical Christian scholar.

Scott, Latayne Colvett. *The Mormon Mirage*. Grand Rapids: Zondervan, 1979.
The author, an active Mormon for ten years before her conversion to Christianity in 1973, explains "the tragedy of Mormonism." Mrs. Scott clearly outlines the teachings of Mormonism and the differences between Mormonism and Christianity.

Smith, Joseph, Jr. *Book of Mormon*. Salt Lake City, UT: The Church of Jesus Christ of Latter-day Saints.

Smith, Joseph, Jr. *Doctrine and Covenants*. Salt Lake City, UT: The Church of Jesus Christ of Latter-day Saints.

Smith, Joseph, Jr. *The Pearl of Great Price*. Salt Lake City, UT: The Church of Jesus Christ of Latter-day Saints, 1957.

Whalen, William J. *The Latter-Day Saints in the Modern Day World*. Notre Dame: University of Notre Dame Press, 1979.
This very interesting book by a Catholic journalist relates the history, teachings, organization, and

splinter groups of the Mormon church. He presents the facts and leaves refutations to the reader.

Tape

Martin, Walter. "The Maze of Mormonism." Santa Ana, CA: Vision House, 1974.

Films

Mormon missionaries are willing to show these films free of charge.

"Man's Search for Happiness." Provo, UT: Brigham Young University, 1964.
This film was used in the Mormon Pavilion of the New York World's Fair. It gives the Mormon view of where we came from, why we are here, and where we go after death. Color. Fourteen minutes.

"Meet the Mormons." Provo, UT: Brigham Young University, 1973.
This introduces the non-Mormon to the Mormon church and its activities. Color. Twenty-four minutes.

4

Christian Science

The seal of the First Church of Christ, Scientist symbolizes victory over sin and disease.

If you've ever received a telegram or letter containing news which was upsetting, you will empathize with Mary in the following illustration. During the summer after her graduation from high school, Mary was separated from her fiancé Frank, who had volunteered for a summer outreach program in another city. While they were apart, Mary felt lonesome and hoped for a letter every day. Weekends were especially difficult for her, and she was very pleased when a letter arrived one Saturday morning. Opening the letter, she discovered a brief message, neatly typed. "Dear Mary," the letter began, "I have never hated to write anything as much as I hate to write this letter. But I want to be honest and let you know that being away from you has made me realize I don't want to be tied down to any one person. I've decided it's best if we split. I know this will hurt, but please try to understand. I'll return your things in three weeks, when I get home." Underneath his typed name were these words: "P. S.

Please don't try to call. I'll be on a retreat till Tuesday."

We would expect Mary to react to such a letter with tears, bitterness, anger, self-pity, guilt, or depression. But let's analyze four aspects of her response. How would she respond physically, emotionally, spiritually, and socially?

A typical response to unsettling news is to have a good cry. Blood pressure rises, pulse rate quickens, the face flushes, and tears flow. Mary would probably feel somewhat relieved and comforted if she were to cry. Her tears would be an outward, physical expression of her emotional response—feelings of hurt, rejection, worthlessness, sorrow, and anger.

A deeper level of Mary's reaction could be called spiritual. For example, Mary might feel guilty, fearing that something she had done caused the breakup. She might even blame God for allowing such a sad thing to happen. Certainly she would be tempted to feel bitterness and resentment toward Frank.

Another reaction could be labeled social. Refusing to talk to anyone, wanting to be left alone, or losing interest in activities would all indicate alienation caused by the letter. Mary's relations with her friends and family might be disrupted.

Conceivably, the physical, emotional, spiritual, and social reactions could snowball if unresolved. Prolonged stress can cause headaches, loss of appetite, ulcers, hives—even conditions severe enough to require hospitalization. Emotional stress can induce irrational behavior or mental breakdown. Exaggerated guilt and self-blame can weaken or debilitate a person. Some people become recluses, unable to rebuild their lives after a shock. If Mary would react severely to the letter, her life could be shattered.

Now suppose that Mary learned a few days later that the letter she'd received was a nasty trick, a cruel hoax, that Frank knew nothing about. He loved her as much as ever, and he was counting the days until they could be together again. Mary would probably feel bewildered and puzzled at first, but then the good news would sink in. Mary's knowledge that the first message was false would reverse all the processes we traced. Physically, Mary would feel better. She would stop grieving and begin to relax. She might whisper a prayer of thanks to God and enjoy heightened appreciation for Frank's love and friendship. Her peace and serenity would return. No longer preoccupied with the sad message, she would be able to resume social activities with vigor.

According to Christian Scientists, this illustration depicts what happens in our lives daily. Christian Science teaches that we constantly receive contradictory messages. If we call the first message *mortal mind*, we can say that mortal mind constantly sends us evil messages. Any message of imperfection is sent by mortal mind. Examples of such messages are: sickness is real, evil is real, hatred is real, sin is real. All messages from mortal mind are cruel hoaxes. If we believe mortal mind, all sorts of problems develop, similar to the physical, emotional, spiritual, and social hurts Mary felt while she thought the first letter was true. All such pain lies within the power of mortal mind.

Christian Science teaches that you can open yourself to a second message. This message is called *immortal Mind*, and it informs you, first and foremost, that mortal mind is nothing but an illusion. If you listen and react to mortal mind, you will experience the *illusions* of doubt, depression, sickness, pain, anger, and sadness. So you must reject the messages of mortal mind. If mortal mind tells you that evil exists in your life, don't listen. Instead, listen to the message of immortal Mind, which informs you that nothing imperfect exists in God's creation. If mortal mind sends a message telling you how sick you feel, reject it. Pay attention only to immortal Mind, which instructs you that sickness is unreal. Let's attempt to clarify this not-so-simple way of looking at life.

Suppose that on Monday morning, you wake up with what seems to be a headache. If you accept this message of mortal mind, you'll likely switch the alarm off and moan in misery. You might exaggerate the symptoms just a bit, convince yourself that you have a touch of the flu, and call off all activities for the day. When this happens, you have accepted the message of mortal mind; you have even cooperated with mortal mind by telling yourself how ill you feel. You probably will feel miserable because, according to Christian Science, you have allowed mortal mind to convince you of a false message.

You might, on the other hand, awaken on Monday feeling under the weather, but reject the message of mortal mind. Instead you listen to immortal Mind, which tells you, "Disregard the first message; it is false."

The basic message of immortal Mind is condensed into two syllogisms: First, all that exists is God, and God is good; therefore all that exists and all that can be experienced is good. Second, all that exists is God, and God is Spirit; therefore all that is real, all that exists, all that can be experienced is Spirit. The one meaning of these two syllogisms is: *Only that exists which is both good and spiritual*. As *Science and Health*, a key scripture of Christian Science, states:

Man is never sick, for Mind is not sick and matter cannot be. A false belief is both the tempter and the tempted, the sin and the sinner, the disease and its cause. It is well to be calm in sickness; to be hopeful is still better; but to understand that sickness is not real and that Truth can destroy its seeming reality, is best of all, for this understanding is the universal and perfect remedy.[1]

Using this message of immortal Mind, you must reject the idea of a headache, because headaches are neither good nor spiritual. According to Christian Science, you should jump out of bed and rush to the bathroom to brush your teeth, telling your-

1. Mary Baker Eddy, *Science and Health with Key to the Scriptures* (Boston: Published by the trustees under the will of Mary Baker Eddy, 1875), pp. 394–395.

self all the while how well you feel. By doing this, you will achieve victory over mortal mind, and as a result you'll find yourself feeling much better than you did before.

When confronted with such an unusual way of looking at experience, many people find these ideas impractical. Perhaps a study of the origins of the ideas and a review of the philosophy underlying them will help us to understand them.

The Origins of Christian Science

The Life of Mary Baker Eddy

The founder of Christian Science, Mary Baker Eddy (1821–1910), struggled with the question of human infirmity throughout her life. During the first half of her nearly ninety years, she searched broadly for spiritual and physical fulfillment. During the last half of her life, she consolidated her discovery that the Bible, rightly understood, provides the solution to human suffering.

Mary Baker Eddy was born and reared on a farm near Concord, New Hampshire. Her childhood was difficult because of poor health and religious confusion. Mary was often ill and unable to attend school. Frail from birth, she contracted an extraordinary number of childhood diseases and was plagued by an anemialike weakness throughout adolescence. But she was a bright child who sought to educate herself, relying on books brought home from the university by her brother Albert. Her curiosity gave rise to unresolved religious questions.

Mary's father was of little help; Mary soon realized that she disagreed with almost everything he believed. A devout Congregationalist, Mr. Baker maintained rigid belief in a radical Calvinism which failed to recognize the love of God and gave untempered support to predestination, election, the wrath of God against the unsaved, and the eternal punishment of hell for the nonelect. Through repeated arguments with her father, Mary realized that she admired his logic but deplored his lack of compassion. Some people have conjectured that Mary's unhappy experiences, continuing into adulthood, left her with a greater need for compassion than for logic, and that this need explains why she spurned her father's beliefs.

After Mary wed in her early twenties, her troubles continued. Her husband died of yellow fever less than a year after their marriage. Poor health prevented her from caring for her only child. Ten years later, she married a dentist, Dr. Patterson, but this marriage compounded her problems when he proved unfaithful. Eventually they were divorced.

The physical and mental strains of Mary's life drove her to seek out Phineas Quimby, a mental healer and mesmerist from Portland, Maine. Mary was intrigued by his method of healing, which he called "the Science of Christ." When she submitted to his practice of hypnotism and mind control, she found mental and physical relief. Excited by her discovery, she soon adopted his beliefs and announced with joy that Jesus' secret of healing had been discovered! The extent to which Quimby influenced Mary is the subject of considerable controversy. Although Mary started a healing career of her own after being trained by Quimby, she had not yet reached the major turning point of her life.

The crisis in Mary's life occurred in 1866, less than two months after Quimby died. Walking down an icy sidewalk, Mary slipped and severely injured her back. Bedridden and in pain, she turned to the Bible account of Jesus healing a paralytic man. As she read, an overpowering desire to believe prompted her to get out of bed. As she acted on the basis of faith in healing, she was able to walk and claimed an eventual healing. Although skeptics have questioned the severity of her injury and the extent of her "divine and miraculous healing," Mary marked this date in 1866 as the beginning of Christian Science and the promised coming of Jesus Christ. Later in life, she described her spiritual breakthrough:

Thus it was when the moment arrived of the heart's bridal to more spiritual existence. When the door opened, I was waiting and watching; and, lo, the bridegroom came! The character of the Christ was illuminated by the midnight torches of Spirit. My heart knew its Redeemer. He whom my affections had diligently sought was as the One "altogether lovely," as "the chiefest," the only "among ten thousand." Soulless famine had fled. Agnosticism, pantheism, and theosophy were void. Being was beautiful, its substance, cause, and currents were

God and His idea. I had touched the hem of Christian Science.[2]

Following this experience, Mary Baker Eddy consolidated her thoughts and beliefs. Through several years of Bible study and searching, she gradually established her beliefs as the principles of spiritual healing. She routinely developed revolutionary interpretations of the Bible, which she compiled in an aptly-named companion book to the Bible, *Science and Health with Key to the Scriptures*. According to Christian Science, study of this book enables its readers to unlock the hidden teachings of the Bible. Today, people in fifty-six countries and 3,200 branches of Christian Science regard her book as indispensable.

Philosophical Influences

As we observed earlier, Phineas Quimby may have played an important role in shaping the thoughts and beliefs of Mary Baker Eddy. We now need to examine the philosophy behind the ideas of Quimby and others like him. This search takes us to Francis Lieber (1800–1872), a German philosopher who came to the University of South Carolina at the age of twenty-seven. Lieber became famous as a philosopher and political mastermind whose ideas strongly influenced international law and civil liberty. He was also the first

2. Mary Baker Eddy, *Retrospection and Introspection* (Boston: Published by the trustees under the will of Mary Baker Eddy, 1920), p. 23.

editor of the *Encyclopedia Americana*. Of special concern to us is Lieber's interest in the German philosopher G. F. Hegel, who wrote a number of articles and books in the early 1800s. While a study of Hegel is too involved for our purposes, we can identify certain Hegelian ideas which Lieber sought to incorporate into a system of truth.

1. There is no truth, substance, life, or intelligence in matter; all is Infinite Mind.
2. Matter has no reality; it is but a manifestation of spirit.
3. There are two basic truths: The Allness of God and the nothingness of matter.
4. God is not personal, because that implies matter; God is more like an impersonal Principle.
5. Only when one is controlled by Love, by Spirit, by Principle—not by physical senses—will one become perfect, immortal, harmonious, and whole.

If you have studied world religions, you've probably noticed a resemblance between the beliefs of Hegel and Lieber, and the Hindu idea of *maya*. Maya is sensory information that tricks people into believing that day-to-day experiences are real. This is an illusion which must be corrected. As long as people are held captive by their illusions, they cannot, according to Hinduism, experience union with Brahman, an impersonal Eternal Essence which is Allness, the only true reality. Perhaps you detect a correspondence between maya and mortal mind, as well as a similarity between Brahman and immortal Mind.

There is a striking similarity between the ideas Lieber and Quimby explored and the concepts of Christian Science as taught by Mary Baker Eddy. This is a serious problem, because Mary Baker Eddy claimed that her ideas were revealed in some divine way:

> I should blush to write of 'Science and Health with Key to the Scriptures' as I have, were it of human origin, and were I, apart from God, its author. But as I was only a scribe echoing the harmonies of heaven in divine metaphysics, I cannot be super-modest in my estimate of the Christian Science textbook.[3]

To explain this, some people have accused Mary Baker Eddy of flagrant dishonesty, but this seems out of character for a sincere seeker of truth. Others, primarily Christian Scientists, agree that some similarity exists between the two works, but insist that Mary Baker Eddy's teachings go far beyond those of Lieber and are basically different. Still others, desiring to be charitable, have concluded that Mary Baker Eddy's anguished attempt to resolve the problem of human suffering blurred her view of the boundary between reality and fantasy.

Our study of the philosophic basis of Christian Science has shown that many ideas came together to produce the insights and beliefs of Mary Baker

3. Mary Baker Eddy, *The First Church of Christ, Scientist, and Miscellany* (Boston: Published by the trustees under the will of Mary Baker Eddy, 1941), p. 115.

Eddy. As we shall observe, the teachings of Christian Science reflect her conclusions.

Christian Science Beliefs

One of the difficulties we confront in a study of Christian Science is the meaning of key biblical concepts. Because Mary Baker Eddy interpreted the Bible spiritually, a person of Christian background might initially find the beliefs of Christian Science agreeable. Further study, however, indicates that the words and ideas of Christian Science denote beliefs radically different from those of historic Christianity. To illustrate this, we will first read a Christian Science statement of belief. Then, in our examination of specific beliefs, we will note the ways Christian Science explains these beliefs.

The basic tenets of Christian Science are six statements which form the "creed" of Christian Science.

1. As adherents of Truth, we take the inspired Word of the Bible as our sufficient guide to eternal Life.
2. We acknowledge and adore one supreme and infinite God. We acknowledge His Son, one Christ; the Holy Ghost or divine Comforter; and man in God's image and likeness.
3. We acknowledge God's forgiveness of sin in the destruction of sin and the spiritual understanding that casts out evil as unreal. But the

belief in sin is punished so long as the belief lasts.

4. We acknowledge Jesus' atonement as the evidence of divine, efficacious Love, unfolding man's unity with God through Christ Jesus the Way-shower; and we acknowledge that man is saved through Christ, through Truth, Life, and Love as demonstrated by the Galilean Prophet in healing the sick and overcoming sin and death.

5. We acknowledge that the crucifixion of Jesus and his resurrection served to uplift faith to understand eternal Life, even the allness of Soul, Spirit, and the nothingness of matter.

6. And we solemnly promise to watch, and pray for that Mind to be in us which was also in Christ Jesus; to do unto others as we would have them do unto us; and to be merciful, just, and pure.[4]

The Nature of God

According to Mary Baker Eddy's spiritual interpretation of the Bible, God is not a personal, caring God. Rather, He is a divine Principle, an impersonal Absolute. God is Allness, Love, Mind, Truth, Soul, Spirit, and Life. Allness means that nothing whatever exists in reality which is not God. Only that which is Love, Mind, Truth, Soul, Spirit, and Life is God. Anything which falls outside of these categories of God is unreal and non-

4. Mary Baker Eddy, *Science and Health with Key to the Scriptures*, p. 497.

existent. God may be defined as "divine Mind," "divine Principle," or, to recall a phrase introduced earlier, "immortal Mind." Note how Mrs. Eddy's explanation of the name *Christian Science* describes the Real (God) and the unreal (matter).

> I named it *Christian*, because it is compassionate, helpful, and spiritual. God I called *immortal Mind*. That which sins, suffers, and dies, I named *mortal mind*. The physical sense, or sensuous nature, I called *error* and *shadow*. Soul I denominated *substance*, because Soul alone is truly substantial. God I characterized as individual entity, but His corporeality I denied. The real I claimed as eternal; and its antipodes, or the temporal, I described as unreal. Spirit I called the *reality*; and matter, the *unreality*.[5]

Quite obviously, this leads to a question, "How can God be the Creator, if the material world is an illusion?" According to Christian Science, Genesis 1 teaches that God created human beings in His own image and likeness, and that He pronounced all that He had made "very good." If humans reflect the image of God (Spirit) they must be completely spiritual and perfect, as is the Creator. If God is Spirit, Love, and Truth, then human identity and reality are the same. Thus it follows that the sick and the sinning mortal human that appears to the physical senses is a false representation; it is a material misconception of humanity.

The Christian concept of God as triune clearly has no place in Christian Science. Mrs. Eddy, who

5. Eddy, *Retrospection and Introspection*, p. 25.

viewed the Jehovah of the Old Testament as a tribal God of war, taught that Jesus revealed God as a spiritual Principle of Love, but His teaching was not perceived until the advent of Christian Science. To describe Christ's role, Mrs. Eddy called Jesus the Way-shower, one who shows the correct way to conceive of God. With regard to the Holy Spirit, Mrs. Eddy claimed that Jesus' promise in John 14:16 was fulfilled when Christian Science arrived. As we saw earlier, the coming of Christian Science coincided with the second advent of Jesus.

Utilizing her spiritual interpretation of the Bible, Mrs. Eddy taught that

> Life, Truth and Love constitute the triune Person called God ... the same in essence, though multiform in office; God the Father-Mother; Christ the spiritual idea of sonship; divine Science or the Holy Comforter. These three express in divine Science the threefold, essential nature of the infinite.[6]

According to Christian Science, belief in God as immortal Mind or divine Principle has major significance for one's personal spiritual and physical well-being. "Ignorance of God, the divine Principle, produces apparent discord, and the right understanding of Him restores harmony."[7]

Christian Scientists admit that one of the reasons for placing special emphasis on spiritual healing is that it provides the most conspicuous

6. Eddy, *Science and Health*, pp. 331–332.
7. *Ibid.*, p. 390.

proof of the validity of the Christian Science understanding of God. Healing is one of the natural results of drawing close to immortal Mind and resolving spiritual conflicts. Note how David's experience appears to support this: "When I kept silent, my bones wasted away through my groaning all day long" (Ps. 32:3). A proper understanding of God, it is believed, restores physical health. But the meaning of the word *healing* in Christian Science goes beyond physical healing to the healing of family problems, psychological tensions, spiritual guilt, and moral confusion. Let's briefly examine the way this works in the life of a Christian Scientist and then review some case histories of spiritual healing.

Because sickness and evil are not real, medical procedures are of little value. When Christian Scientists become ill, or are so informed by mortal mind, they immediately conclude that their understanding of Reality—God—has been disturbed. By seeking spiritual renewal or regeneration, they try to reject the false message of mortal mind. An intense desire to understand God correctly must be the motive. They must not want to be cured because of pain; that would be a concession to mortal mind and an inadequate motive for healing.

Christian Scientists customarily seek healing two ways. They usually respond to the messages of mortal mind by turning immediately to *Science and Health* and reading some of the helpful truths which affirm that God is real and evil is not. They may seek assistance from Christian Science practitioners or nurses, full-time counselors who approach human problems from a perspective of Christian Science. Spiritual assistance is offered by phone, home visits, or office calls.

Another way to respond is through prayer, usually prayers of affirmation or prayerful thoughts which reflect on the nature of God, immortal Mind. For example, a Christian Scientist might pray, "Infinite God of Supreme Goodness, since you have created only what is Good and I am your Perfect Child, let me accept my wholeness and my perfection as your creation." Both these responses are exemplified in testimonies such as those to which we will soon turn.

We could summarize the Christian Science understanding of God in this way: If we can overcome the unreal messages of mortal mind and affirm the reality of immortal Mind alone, our well-being will increase physically, spiritually, emotionally, and socially. Mrs. Eddy herself realized the significance of this view of God, for she wrote,

> What is the cardinal point of the difference in my metaphysical system? This: that *by knowing the unreality of disease, sin, and death*, you demonstrate the allness of God. This difference wholly separates my system from all others. The reality of these so-called existences I deny, because they are not to be found in God, and this system is built on Him as the sole cause. It would be difficult to name any previous teachers, save Jesus and his apostles, who have thus taught.[8]

8. Mary Baker Eddy, *Unity of Good* (Boston: Published by the trustees under the will of Mary Baker G. Eddy, 1936), pp. 9–10.

Teachings about Christ

Because Christian Science uses traditional Christian terms to teach abstract philosophical concepts unfamiliar to evangelical Christians, Christian Science teachings about Christ are elusive and confusing. Christian Science doctrines, stated in familiar, traditional words, describe Jesus as the perfect example of what it means to be the Son of God. Jesus is considered our Savior, our Way-shower. Christian Science accords Jesus the highest place in human history. These concepts seem familiar to evangelical Christians (with the exception, perhaps, of Jesus' title, Way-shower). But further study uncovers the fact that Christian Science uses traditional words to convey new, indistinct ideas. Examination of a few concepts will illustrate the ambiguity of Christian Science descriptions of the person and the work of Christ.

Evangelical Christians believe that Jesus Christ came to earth in human form, assumed a human nature, and lived an incarnate, mortal life. But what does this mean when interpreted by the Christian Science view of mortal existence?

> The sensual cannot be made the mouthpiece of the spiritual, nor can the finite become the channel of the infinite.[9]

> If a material body — in other words, mortal material sense — were permeated by Spirit, that body would disappear to mortal sense, would be deathless.[10]

9. Eddy, *Science and Health*, p. 73.
10. *Ibid.*, p. 72.

The concept of Christ assuming a human nature is further confused by the Christian Science understanding of humanity.

What is man? Man is not matter; he is not made up of brain, blood, bones, and other material elements. The Scriptures inform us that man is made in the image and likeness of God. Matter is not that likeness. . . . Man is spiritual and perfect; and because he is spiritual and perfect, he must be so understood in Christian Science. Man is idea, the image, of Love; he is not physique.[11]

Evangelical Christians teach that Jesus as the Christ suffered and died for the unsaved. But Mary Baker Eddy states:

In Science, Christ never died. In material sense Jesus died, and lived. The fleshly Jesus seemed to die, though he did not.[12]

Jesus experienced few of the pleasures of the physical senses, but his sufferings were the fruits of other people's sins, not of his own. The eternal Christ, his spiritual selfhood, never suffered. Jesus mapped out the path for others. He unveiled the Christ, the spiritual idea of divine Love.[13]

If you asked evangelical Christians, "What does Jesus save us from?" most would quickly respond, "From our sins." How then do we understand the unreality of sin as described in *Science and Health*?

11. *Ibid.*, p. 475.
12. Eddy, *Unity of Good*, p. 62.
13. Eddy, *Science and Health*, p. 38.

Nothing is real and eternal,—nothing is Spirit,—
but God and His idea. Evil has no reality. It is
neither person, place, nor thing, but is simply a
belief, an illusion of material sense.[14]

Obviously, Christian Science considers sin a
mental delusion, whereas evangelical Christians
regard sin as specific acts of disobedience to God.

Note how the following extended passage from
Science and Health uses traditional Christian
terms and ideas while reinterpreting the person
of Christ, His virgin birth, and His life in the state
of humiliation as Jesus.

Jesus was born of Mary. Christ is the true idea
voicing good, the divine message from God to men
speaking to the human consciousness. The Christ
is incorporeal, spiritual,—yea, the divine image
and likeness, dispelling the illusions of the senses;
the Way, the Truth, and the Life, healing the sick
and casting out evils, destroying sin, disease, and
death. As Paul says: "There is one God, and one
mediator between God and men, the man Christ
Jesus." The corporeal man Jesus was human.

Jesus demonstrated Christ; he proved that Christ
is the divine idea of God—the Holy Ghost, or Comforter, revealing the divine Principle, Love, and
leading into all truth.

Jesus was the son of a virgin. He was appointed
to speak God's word and to appear to mortals in
such a form of humanity as they could understand
as well as perceive. Mary's conception of him was
spiritual, for only purity could reflect Truth and
Love, which were plainly incarnate in the good

14. *Ibid.*, p. 71.

and pure Christ Jesus. He expressed the highest
type of divinity, which a fleshly form could express
in that age. Into the real and ideal man the fleshly
element cannot enter. Thus it is that Christ illustrates the coincidence, or spiritual agreement,
between God and man in His image.[15]

Such ambiguous uses of traditional Christian
terms abound in the writings of Mary Baker Eddy.
And although leaders of Christian Science differ
sharply with his appraisal, many who explore
Christian Science share the conclusion of
Anthony A. Hoekema:

... Christian Science denies the unity of the Person of Jesus Christ, Jesus' present existence, the
absolute necessity for Jesus' earthly mission, the
incarnation of Christ, the Virgin birth of Jesus, the
sinlessness of Jesus, the full deity of Jesus, and
Jesus' genuine humanity. In addition, they reject
Jesus' suffering, death, physical resurrection, and
ascension into heaven. By what conceivable right,
therefore, do the members of this group still dare
to call themselves a church of *Christ*?[16]

The Way of Salvation

Previously, this chapter explained the difference between the Christian Science understanding of salvation and that of historic Christianity.
The Christian Scientist believes that sin is a

15. *Ibid.*, pp. 332–333.
16. *The Four Major Cults* (Grand Rapids: Eerdmans, 1963),
p. 207.

shadow, an error of mortal mind, lacking existence. But we still find in the Christian Science understanding of salvation that works are of primary importance, while the grace of God is neglected. For example, if you should ask, "Why follow Christian Science teachings? What's their purpose?" a Christian Scientist's answer would stress human works, more mental than manual.

The aim of Christian Science is deliverance from every form of evil, from all that denies the perfection and goodness inherent in being created in the image of God. To put it directly, if human beings are to overcome sin, sickness, selfishness, ignorance, fear, hedonism, or materialism, they must do so by discovering a new understanding of God as immortal Mind. Salvation comes by right thinking, and right thinking comes by correct comprehension of God. For this reason, Christian Science appeals to intellectual, philosophical people. The Christian Scientists' positive approach to life's problems and their encouragement to develop strong characters and virtuous lives gain many converts. Furthermore, their emphasis on the Bible as God's revealed truth, understood properly, appeals to many. But how do Christian Scientists regard the Bible?

The Bible

Our study of Christian Science beliefs began with a statement of faith which speaks of the Bible as a "sufficient guide" to salvation. We now realize that Mary Baker Eddy spiritualized the teachings of the Bible, but we have not defined "spiritualizing" the Bible. According to Christian Science, "spiritualizing" means ridding the Bible of all material elements which reproduce the messages of mortal mind. When the Bible is read, every page must be interpreted spiritually, not literally or symbolically. As an example of a spiritual interpretation, note the following commentary of John 5:8, written by a Christian Science practitioner:

In the healings Christ Jesus performed he evidently saw through the discordant mortal picture and recognized what is real and true of the man of God's creating—his spiritual perfection as God's likeness. When he came to the man at the pool of Bethesda who had been paralyzed for thirty-eight years, he did not accept the argument that matter could make conditions for the man. He did not accept the belief fixed in the man's thought for the many years he had been incapacitated. Jesus dismissed it with the statement "Rise, take up thy bed, and walk."

The man, no doubt inspired by the Christ, Truth, which Jesus expressed, forgot the self-justification and probably the self-pity he had been clinging to those many years—forgot he lacked something, namely, someone to put him into the pool. The strength of Jesus' spirituality destroyed the belief that the man could not be healed because others were more fortunate than he and could get to the pool. The man arose and walked.[17]

17. Jay Holmes, "It's only a picture," *Christian Science Sentinel*, September 29, 1973, p. 1689.

Mary Baker Eddy cited more than three hundred thousand errors in the New Testament, but observed that historical sections of the Bible have no importance. On the other hand, she insisted that her book, *Science and Health with Key to the Scriptures*, was "unerring and divine." She claimed that using *Science and Health* is the only way to understand the spiritual and correct meaning of the Bible. The Bible can be understood only when it is interpreted spiritually—in other words, by following the guidelines of Mary Baker Eddy's views.

Christian Science Practices

Worship

Sunday worship services are conducted by First and Second Readers, who are male or female members elected from the local church. The readers read a lesson-sermon, composed of related passages in the Bible and *Science and Health*. These lesson-sermons are not designed to be delivered with any particular skill. The content is the important thing and not the manner of delivery. Mrs. Eddy chose twenty-six subjects for these lesson-sermons, which are repeated twice a year. Each member is expected to have studied relevant passages, which are listed prior to the Sunday worship.

On Wednesdays, there are meetings which include testimonies of physical and spiritual healings. At this midweek service, the First Reader reads a lesson of his or her choice.

The Sacraments

Although Christian Scientists recognize two sacraments, baptism and the Lord's Supper, their observance is spiritualized. The sacraments are not treated as outward signs or church rituals at all, but as daily individual experiences. Baptism is the inward purification of thought from all error. It is meant to lead to a regeneration and cleansing of character, and will consequently improve individual behavior. The Lord's Supper is observed twice a year as a silent, inner process of opening oneself to the presence of God by meditation on the example of Jesus, the Way-shower. Each person worships or simply kneels in silent communion with God. In view of the constant emphasis on spiritualizing all of life, it is not surprising that Christian Scientists use no visible elements in either sacrament.

Prayer

Praise and supplication to God have little place in Christian Science, because prayer does not affect an impersonal Principle. As a result, prayer consists of concentration on divine truth or meditation on immortal Mind. It is regarded as a means of affirming the only realities: Love, Mind, Spirit, and Truth. Prayer helps rid one of mortal mind and realigns one with a proper realization that immortal Mind alone is real.

Spiritual Healing

Christian Science services, as well as church periodicals, regularly include testimonies of healings which members have experienced. The following two accounts closely resemble experiences reported by members. Although these accounts are fictional and for illustration only, you can read similar firsthand accounts in the *Christian Science Sentinel*.

While I was putting storm windows on our house, I slipped off the ladder and fell about eight feet to the ground. I landed on my left foot, and when I tried to stand up, my ankle gave out. A friend, who had been helping me with the windows, thought I had broken it. He helped me into the house, where we put ice on my foot. By that evening, my ankle was swollen to twice its normal size. I felt pain from my knee to my toes. Trying to stand on it was out of the question. My friend called a neighbor, who was a knowledgeable Christian Scientist. The neighbor told me that as a child of God, I was a perfect being, and that I should repeat that truth to myself. The next morning, I tried to stand on my foot, but the pain was intense. I went back to bed discouraged. That evening our neighbor again came to see how I was doing. She told me about Mrs. Eddy's statement that God's child is the same before a bone is broken as after. We prayed together, and as she left I realized that my ankle hurt only because I was accepting the material evidence that it was injured. I knew then that the only thing that could interfere with my harmony as a child of God was my own negative thinking. I went to sleep with a feeling of peace. The next morning I got up and went to work with no pain whatever!

In the months since this experience, I have been healthy and free from worry. I have become aware of the nothingness of matter and the allness of God, and have realized that I am a perfect creature as God's child.

Science and Health has completely changed my life. The day after my husband and I returned from a vacation seventeen years ago, I became very ill. This was nothing new for me, because I had been sick for much of my adult life and had submitted to several surgeries. Pain and fever kept me in bed for a week. After witnessing a severe attack of pain, my husband took me to the emergency room, where the doctor diagnosed a serious kidney infection and said that he wanted to admit me. When I refused to enter the hospital, the doctor wrote me a prescription for a powerful antibiotic. Then my husband took me home.

My husband asked his mother to stay with me until I felt better. Fortunately, his mother had recently begun to study Christian Science. She asked if I would like to be visited by a Christian Science practitioner. How thankful I am today that I agreed! When the practitioner came, she read to me from *Science and Health* and explained Mrs. Eddy's discovery that matter is nothing and that physical circumstances are powerless to destroy our harmony as God's children. She told me that sickness is unreal, because it was not created or intended by God. She told me also that God loves His children, and that if I could deny the existence of matter, I would realize that I was not sick, but was well and harmonious. By the next day, my pain was gone, even though I had stopped taking medication. I was completely well before the week ended. I have not been ill since.

Today, many dedicated families rely solely on Christian Science for all their health needs. It is their experience that not some but *all* bodily ills are mental in origin. And they cite the increased awareness of psychosomatic illnesses in recent years as newly-acquired proof that the bodily illness, hatred, lust, fear, and doubt of our human existence can only be eliminated by spiritual means. This emphasis on spiritual healing, so central to the Christian Science way of life, has recently placed the church at the center of a growing controversy.

Douglas and Rita Swan, both faculty members at Jamestown College in North Dakota, were reared in Christian Science families. When their sixteen-month-old son, Matthew, contracted meningitis, he was treated by a Christian Science practitioner. Believing that reliance on medicine shuts off God's help and breaks the commandment against false gods, the Swans did not seek medical attention for Matthew. Asking the Swans to only be patient, trusting, and humble, the practitioner never suggested medical treatment as Matthew's condition worsened. Within two weeks, Matthew died.

The Swans withdrew their membership and sued the Church of Christ, Scientist and two of its practitioners for negligence in Matthew's death. They claimed that Christian Science membership qualifications include a pledge not to use medicine. They also alleged that church leaders forbid practitioners to give spiritual treatment to members who voluntarily accept medical help. These sanctions, the Swans insisted, restrain Christian Science parents from seeking medical help and deprive children of their legal rights.

After presenting her story on "The Phil Donahue Show," Mrs. Swan received more than 180 reports alleging death and injury to Christian Science children deprived of medical treatment. Awareness of these cases led Mrs. Swan to protest a government code which states that a parent who does not provide medical treatment for a child because of religious beliefs will not be considered a negligent parent. This regulation of the United States Department of Health and Human Services, now incorporated into many state laws, seems to imply that Christian Science parents who deprive their sick children of medication or treatment cannot be charged with child abuse or neglect. The code does state that courts can order medical services in life-threatening situations over the protest of parents. But Christian Science members, who are taught to disbelieve in disease and illness, fail to recognize and report serious symptoms or life-threatening illness in their children.

Of course, the Christian Science church is not the only church involved in lawsuits of this nature. Many faith-healing sects discourage members from seeking medical care and urge them on to a greater reliance on divine healing. Some religious groups object to programs of immunization; others urge followers to discontinue prescribed medications as proof of their faith in the power of God to heal. But the central role of divine healing in the Christian Science way of life will likely make it more vulnerable to lawsuits and unfavorable publicity. Regardless of the outcome of these cases, Mary Baker Eddy committed

121

Christian Science believers to a denial of the existence of disease and to the practice of divine healing.

All of this doesn't mean that Christian Scientists never seek medical help. Although the faith claims healing for a wide range of illnesses, including bone fractures, members of Christian Science churches haven't always attained a high enough degree of understanding and spiritual perception, and thus desire medical attention. The church treats these members sympathetically, while encouraging them to improve their spiritual understanding and employ Christian Science methods exclusively to demonstrate a higher commitment and greater consistency in their practice of Christian Science.

The Organization of Christian Science

Church Government

Mary Baker Eddy devised a system of church government, the *Church Manual*, which is still adhered to. A board of directors, composed of five faithful members, administers the affairs of the Mother Church located in Boston. Each local branch of the church is governed democratically in all aspects except those covered by the *Church Manual*. Until a local group gathers more than fifty members, it is called a Christian Science Society, an organized branch which has not yet met the requirements for becoming a church.

Christian Science fellowships are also located on many college and university campuses.

Reading Rooms

Christian Scientists are not aggressively evangelistic. They provide reading rooms so that inquirers may study their literature. Each congregation, whether consisting of fifty or five hundred members, is expected to provide a reading room in its geographical area. Each reading room supplies ample biographies of Mary Baker Eddy, even though she is not worshiped in any sense.

Questions

1. What is the appeal of Christian Science? Do you think certain types of personalities would be more attracted than others? If so, what types?
2. Write a two-page script of an imaginary conversation between Job and Mary Baker Eddy.
3. Read John 20:24–31. Which specific events in this resurrection appearance of Christ do not correspond with Christian Science teachings?
4. In a book about early church history, locate a description of the Gnostics. Which elements of their beliefs do you find in Christian Science? Which books of the Bible were apparently written in opposition to the Gnostics?
5. Read Matthew 1:23; Luke 1:35; Romans 1:3–4; 8:3; I Corinthians 1:30; Galatians 4:4–5; I Timothy 3:16; Hebrews 2:9, 14–17; 4:15; I Peter 3:18, 21-22; I John

5:20. How do these passages compare with Christian Science teachings?

6. Some people call cults "the unpaid bills of the church," because they think that each cult fills a vacuum within the Christian church. With regard to Christian Science, this would be a criticism of the church for neglecting the spiritual dimension of healing. Is this criticism legitimate? Why, or why not?

7. In *The Four Major Cults* (see chapter 7 for details), Anthony Hoekema lists four general suggestions for dealing with a cult member:

show genuine love

show humility

recognize the lessons that a Christian can learn from the cult

know the cult's teachings, and be fair and do not distort those teachings when you discuss them with a cult member

Which of these methods do you think would be most effective for approaching a Christian Scientist? Why?

Additional Sources of Information

Books

Eddy, Mary Baker. *Science and Health with Key to the Scriptures*. Boston: First Church of Christ, Scientist, 1875.

Hoekema, Anthony A. *Christian Science*. Grand Rapids: Eerdmans, 1974.
A scholarly study of the theology of Christian Science from a biblical perspective. This book is also a chapter in his book, *The Four Major Cults* (Eerdmans, 1963).

Leishman, Thomas Lenton. *Why I Am a Christian Scientist*. New York: Thomas Nelson, 1958.
An interesting account of the Christian Science movement, its founders, and organization. This book is no longer in print, but is available at Christian Science reading rooms.

Martin, Walter. *The Kingdom of the Cults*. Grand Rapids: Zondervan, 1965.
The chapter about Christian Science contains an interesting documented account of the sources of many of Mrs. Eddy's ideas.

Tape

Martin, Walter. "Healing: Devilish or Divine." Santa Ana, CA: Vision House, 1974.

5

First Unification Church

The sun figures prominently in the symbol of the First Unification Church, representing the messiah who came from the east, the land of the rising sun.

You find them in shopping malls, supermarket parking lots, airports, and residential areas. They sell flowers, peanuts, or candy. They've also been known to sell Avis "We Try Harder" buttons (which they picked up free) for a two-dollar donation. They gladly accept food stamps and personal checks.

The smiling solicitors claim to represent a variety of causes. The following statements are common: "I'm raising funds for our camp for the rehabilitation of young people." "We're asking you to help us in a Christian youth ministry." "Our church has just bought a camp from the YMCA. Lots of kids can't afford to go, so could you help us send a kid to our camp?" "We're part of the One World Crusade, and we need your help."

What you will not be told is that the solicitors are from the First Unification Church, which operates no known charitable organization, and that your donation will end up in the treasury of

127

Sun Myung Moon's new mission to the world. If you should question the solicitors, you will not likely be told the truth, since lying for their Master is not wrong; it's merely "using heavenly deception." Who is this man who has recently made such an impact in North America?

The Origin of the First Unification Church

The Life of Sun Myung Moon

Yong Myung Moon, the second of eight children, was born in 1920 to a Korean farm family and reared in a small village in what is now North Korea. Young Moon attended a local Presbyterian church until his parents sent him to high school in Seoul, Korea. There he found the Pentecostal church to his liking, largely because it accommodated his flamboyant personality.

Moon claims that at the age of sixteen, he withdrew to a spot in the Korean mountains to pray and meditate on Easter Sunday. Mysteriously, Jesus appeared to Moon and told him that he had been selected to finish the work Jesus had been unable to complete. The details of his mission, including a new set of principles and teachings for our generation, were revealed to him directly by God.

After his first revelation, Moon spent nine years reflecting, searching, and waiting for his messianic destiny. Among the poor Buddhists with whom he lived, there were constant whispers that a new Buddha would be born, an embodiment of intense spiritual insight. Even in the Pentecostal church, rumors persisted of a prophecy indicating that a messiah was coming to Korea. After high school, Moon attended a university in Tokyo, Japan, where he studied electrical engineering. On his return to Korea at age twenty-four, Moon became the spiritual leader of a group of Koreans, but his beliefs and teachings had not crystallized.

Perhaps Moon's strong desire for a clear set of beliefs prompted him, at age twenty-six, to enter the Israel Monastery. Here he studied under Korean-born Park Moon Kim, who believed himself to be the new savior of the world. During this period of study, Moon's principles became clearer, and his confidence in his messianic role increased. Two heaven-sent messages were given to him, resulting in a new name to reflect his messianic destiny. The name of his teacher, Park Moon Kim, incorporated his own name *Moon*. Perhaps he interpreted this as God's message, to identify him as the messiah. The name *Park Moon Kim* means "one hundred gold letters." Moon changed his name to Sun Myung Moon, meaning "shining proper letter." Some suggest that the selection indicates that Moon believed his teacher, Kim, was a glowing forerunner to the messiah, but he himself was the *shining* messiah.

Moon founded the Broad Sea Church at age twenty-six. Because he claimed the title of "reverend" and advanced radical, unbiblical teachings, the Presbyterian Church of Korea excommunicated him within two years. What happened to Moon for the next eight years is difficult to determine. We do know that he was a rabid anti-

Communist and was imprisoned by the Communists for some of that time. When the Korean War broke out in the early 1950s, Moon had fled to South Korea, where he remained for the duration of the war.

During this time, Moon was constantly harassed by the authorities and imprisoned more than three times. In an obvious messianic allusion, Moon tells his followers how he was left for dead by the police, who threw his broken body behind the police station. While carrying Moon's corpse away for burial, his friends were startled to find him breathing. Three days later he was preaching. Enough evidence exists for a less glorious explanation that includes imprisonment on charges of adultery, bigamy, and promiscuity. Some confusion exists regarding his married life. Some people claim that he has been married four times, and offer to supply the names of his wives. Moon insists that he was married only once, discounting his first marriage to a woman who failed to be a perfect wife. His current wife is integrally related to Moon's religious concepts.

North Americans were unaware of Moon's teaching until the mid-1970s when Moon, in response to a divine revelation in 1972, emigrated to America as a permanent resident alien. Soon after his arrival, Moon launched his marathon tour, speaking in many major North American cities. Since that time, thousands of young converts have been spreading the teachings of the *Divine Principle*, Moon's bible. Moon's recruitment effort is aimed primarily at disillusioned, confused young people, often on college campuses. Under the guise of organizations such as Sunburst, One World Crusade, New Hope Singers, International, D. C. Striders Track Club, or Korean Folk Ballet, Moon followers lure prospective converts into retreats and communes where they learn to obey the Master. His message appeals primarily to Jews and young people of nominal church background who respect the Bible and believe in God, but are biblically illiterate.

Moon himself lives in luxury in New York State in a twenty-five-room mansion, valued at well over $700,000. For church offices he purchased the forty-two-story New Yorker Hotel for five million dollars. From there Moon's organization directs the mission program of the First Unification Church. Occasionally Moon addresses his followers in a public speech, but he is hampered by a language problem, since he speaks Korean. He relies on his book, *Divine Principle*, his published speeches (*Master Speaks*), his deeply committed followers, and his trained recruits to spread the teachings of the cult. But church members are constantly reminded of the importance of Moon, who confidently claims, "I am your brain," or, "Until now, Jesus appeared in the spirit world to his followers; from now on, I will appear."

The Beliefs of the First Unification Church

While Moon described his earliest revelation as a direct visit from Jesus, the contents of his teachings are supposed to have been received gradually through study, prayer, meditation, and

131

communication with Jesus, Moses, Buddha, and God. Most, but not all, teachings of the Unification Church are included in *Divine Principle*, which claims, "With the fullness of time, God has sent His messenger to resolve the fundamental questions of life and the universe. His name is Sun Myung Moon."[1]

Admitting that Christians can hardly be expected to welcome a new revelation, *Divine Principle* explains that the Bible is not the truth itself, but a textbook teaching the truth, and it must not be accepted as absolute in every detail.

What are the "fundamental questions of life and the universe"? According to *Divine Principle*, the following questions and answers present the core teachings of Moon.

What are the basic beliefs? There are three persons, according to *Divine Principle*, who play a part in God's plan to bring humanity into restored fellowship: the first Adam, the second Adam, and the Lord of the Second Advent. The first Adam was God's first human creation who, with Eve, fell into sin. The second Adam was Jesus, who died on the cross because of the disloyalty of the Jews and John the Baptist, a traitor. The Lord of the Second Advent is the Messiah, who must come to establish the Kingdom of Heaven on earth.

Was Adam created perfect? God created Adam pure and capable of growing to spiritual perfection. God intended Eve to complement Adam and to enable

1. The Unification Church, *Divine Principle* (New York: The Holy Spirit Association for the Unification of World Christianity, 1973), p. 16.

them to grow, but they originally related to each other as a brother and sister. After they grew to maturity as husband and wife, God intended for them to establish a biological family, the Kingdom of Heaven on earth. For centuries, the story of Adam and Eve has been misunderstood.

How then did Adam and Eve sin? As *Divine Principle* presents the account, after God created Adam and Eve, Lucifer (Satan) became troubled by two things: jealousy because God loved Adam and Eve so much, and lust because Eve was sexually attractive. When Lucifer had sexual intercourse with Eve, humanity fell *spiritually*. As soon as Eve realized what she had done, she knew that creation had been desecrated. In fact, she saw, for the first time, that Adam, not Lucifer, was her intended sexual partner. Hoping to regain her lost position, she had sexual intercourse with Adam. This constituted the *physical* fall of humanity.

What resulted from this spiritual and physical fall of human beings? As a result of Eve's intercourse with Lucifer, she delivered a child named Cain, who symbolized the human relationship with Satan. The embodiment of this relationship is Communism. When Eve became pregnant by Adam, she gave birth to Abel, who represented the human relationship with God, now embodied in democracy. Today the son of Satan empowers Communism and the Son of God empowers democracy. As a direct result of the fall, humankind must be restored to God through both a *physical* and a *spiritual* redemption. No one was obedient enough to effect such a redemption until a truly obedient person was born, Jesus of Nazareth.

Who was Jesus? According to *Divine Principle*, Jesus was the second Adam, spoken of by many messengers. In the sixth century B.C., God sent Buddha to India and Confucious to China. In the fifth century

B.C., Socrates was sent to Greece and the prophet Malachi was sent to the Jews. Every religion received a messenger sent by God to prepare the nations for the coming unity under Jesus.

In what sense did Jesus accomplish salvation? If Jesus had not been crucified, he would have found the perfect mate and fathered God's family on earth. This would have accomplished the physical restoration or redemption of sinful humanity. But Satan thwarted Jesus' intention to father the family of God by entering his body, possibly making him incapable of having children. Jesus was crucified before he found the perfect mate. John the Baptist had encouraged the Jews to reject Jesus, because he did not believe that one who came eating and drinking could be the Messiah. When Jesus discovered that he could not accomplish both the physical *and* spiritual salvation of humanity, he opted to complete at least the spiritual redemption, and accepted the cross as the cost of spiritual salvation.

Did Jesus rise from the dead? No. According to *Divine Principle*, his appearances between his death and ascension were appearances of a spirit being, transcending time and space.

Who will accomplish the physical salvation of humanity? The Lord of the Second Advent, who must be born on earth in order to accomplish physical salvation.

Who will this be? Revelation 7:2–3 says, "Then I saw another angel coming up from the east, having the seal of the living God. He called out a loud voice to the four angels who had been given power to harm the land and the sea: 'Do not harm the land or the sea or the trees until we put a seal on the foreheads of the servants of our God.' " Just as the Bible foretold the birthplace of Jesus, this passage foretells the birthplace of the Lord of the Second Advent, who is the other angel. He will come up from the east. *Divine Principle* explains that this could refer to one of three countries: Korea, Japan, or China. China is excluded as a possibility because it is on the satanic side of Communism. Japan is disqualified because it controlled Korea from 1910–1945 and persecuted Christians during this time, especially during World War II. So the birthplace of the Lord of the Second Advent must be Korea.

When will this take place? The number 2,000 provides the clue. Dating from the time of Abraham, it took God 2,000 years to prepare for the coming of Jesus. Similarly, the Lord of the Second Advent will come 2,000 years after Jesus. So the Messiah has probably already been born. This new Messiah will accomplish physical salvation by parenting a new family, crossing all ethnic and religious barriers. This will complete the redemption of humanity and usher in the kingdom of God, the restored spiritual and physical family of God.

No member of the Unification Church openly teaches that Moon is the Messiah. This belief is revealed in *Divine Principle*. The members' strategy calls them to gather the lost into their close-knit fellowship, where each convert will come to a belief in Moon as the Messiah—a belief based on spiritual insight. As we will note, early contacts rarely include any mention of Moon; only after more "advanced spiritual maturity" are converts exposed to him. At such time, they may hear people testify: "Moon is our Father and Master." "Master is more than any saint, prophet, religious leader, or theologian. Master is greater

135

than Jesus Himself." "We are the diseased, Master is the Physician. We must obey Master if we wish to be healed." "Under Master Moon we will conquer the world. We will replace the United Nations."

Unification Beliefs Contrasted with the Bible

Inspiration

The Bible, however, is not the truth itself, but a textbook teaching the truth. Naturally, the quality of teaching and the method and extent of giving the truth must vary according to each age, for the truth is given to people of different ages, who are at different spiritual and intellectual levels. Therefore, we must not regard the textbook as absolute in every detail. [*Divine Principle*, p. 9]

All scripture is God-breathed and is useful for teaching, rebuking, correcting and training in righteousness, so that the man of God may be thoroughly equipped for every good work. [II Tim. 3:16–17]

Every word of God is flawless; he is a shield to those who take refuge in him. Do not add to his words, or he will rebuke you, and prove you a liar. [Prov. 30:5–6]

Contact with the Spirit

If you go on cultivating such experiences, you will reach the point where your heart will be broadened to be a channel of communication with the spirit world. [*Master Speaks*, 2–20–73, p. 7]

Let no one be found among you...who practices divination or sorcery, interprets omens, engages in witchcraft, or casts spells, or who is a medium or spiritist or who consults the dead. Anyone who does these things is detestable to the Lord.... [Deut. 18:10–12a]

Jesus' Divinity

Since it is true that a per-fected man [such as Jesus] is one body with God, "Jesus" may well be called God. Nevertheless, he can by no means be God Himself. [*Divine Principle*, pp. 209–211]

For God was pleased to have all his fulness dwell in him. [Col. 1:19]

Redemption

This is salvation, in Unifica-tion Church. Through Father [Moon] and Mother [his wife] we can be born anew, sin-lessly. [*120-Day Training Manual*, pp. 41–42]

Father [Moon] is given au-thority here on earth by God to forgive sin. [*120-Day Training Manual*, p. 41]

Prayer should be offered to Heavenly Father through True Parents. [*120-Day Training Manual*, p. 203]

There is one God and one mediator between God and men, the man Christ Jesus. [I Tim. 2:5]

...all have sinned and fall short of the glory of God, and are justified freely by his grace, through the redemp-tion that came by Christ Jesus. God presented him as a sacrifice of atonement, through faith in his blood. [Rom. 3:23–25a]

Salvation is found in no one else, for there is no other name under heaven given to men by which we must be saved. [Acts 4:12]

The Suffering Messiah

During my first 3 years of public ministry, just as Jesus did, I had to go through se-vere hardships culminating

But see Jesus...crowned with glory and honor be-cause he suffered death, so that by the grace of God he in the torture of prison life, which was more for me than Jesus' cross.

I had to accomplish all left unaccomplished by my predecessor. ...When you think of that, you must feel indebted to me and you cannot lift your face before me. [*Master Speaks*, 5–27–73, p. 13; 3–4–73, p. 10]

might taste death for everyone. [Heb. 2:9]

For we do not have a high priest who is unable to sympathize with our weaknesses, but we have one who has been tempted in every way, just as we are—yet was without sin. Let us then approach the throne of grace with confidence, so that we may receive mercy and find grace to help us in our time of need. [Heb. 4:15–16]

What Jesus Accomplished

Nothing. There was but one thing left. He died for God and heaven—that is the only thing he accomplished. He died, 'Not my will, but I'll die for God'—that is the only thing he left. Nothing was accomplished, nobody, no disciples at all, nothing, just death. Christianity started after his death anyway. [*Master Speaks*, 7–4–73, p. 3]

For Christ died for sins once for all, the righteous for the unrighteous, to bring you to God. [I Peter 3:18a]

...by one sacrifice he has made perfect forever those who are being made holy. [Heb. 10:14]

A New Messiah?

Then they can understand that Rev. Moon is Messiah, the Lord of the Second Advent.

At that time if anyone says to you, 'Look, here is the Christ!' or 'There he is!' do not believe it. For false Christs and false prophets

If only they can understand the fall of man they can understand that Father is the Messiah.

Father is visible God. [*120-Day Training Manual*, pp. 160, 222, 362]

will appear....For as the lightning comes from the east and flashes to the west, so will be the coming of the Son of Man. [Matt. 24:23–24a, 27]

Come, Lord Jesus. [Rev. 22:20b]

Unification Recruitment Methods

Perhaps the teachings of the Unification Church prompt you to ask, "How could anybody believe Reverend Moon?" Consider the following facts:

1. According to the 1977 Gallup Youth Survey, a whopping 95 percent of American teen-agers believe in God or a Universal Spirit. And 75 percent of these believe in "a personal God who observes a person's actions, and rewards or punishes." More than 900 of the 1,000 interviewed said they pray, and 400 said they pray frequently. Obviously, young people are searching for a relationship with God which produces happiness and assurance. Such people are the eager victims of the Moonies.

2. The First Unification Church accepts the potential convert warmly and quickly, but indoctrinates slowly. All accounts of those returning from the movement tell the same story: "I was surrounded by caring, loving

people." "They were so clean, civilized, just full of pep and energy—always smiling." "It seems they would do anything to make me comfortable and happy." "They really know what they believe and they don't ask questions. They know their place, I mean they know exactly what they believe, and I respected that."

The indoctrination methods of the Unification Church have brought accusations of brainwashing. Some desperate parents have even used physical force to remove their children from the communes they live in. However, this has sometimes created serious legal problems. Such an instance is the story of Tammy Schuppin, whose parents described their battle with Moon's forces in a magazine article.[2]

According to the article, Tammy became involved with the Unification Church between October 1974 and January 1975, dropping out of school and leaving her family. Within nine months, her letters began to take on a strange tone, as though they were written by another person. Her voice on the telephone sounded flat and distant, reminding her parents of the zombielike appearance they had seen in other followers of Moon. As she was about to go to a four-month training session, Tammy's parents decided to gain custody of Tammy by force, and to have her

2. Margaret Bowers, "Sun Myung Moon Has Taken Our Daughter," *Eternity* 27 (April 1976), p. 26.

deprogramed at one of the centers which have sprouted in North America.[3]

Tammy's parents enlisted three friends to help. Their plan was to drive a van to the shopping mall where Tammy was raising funds. As startled shoppers looked on, the three friends forced Tammy into the van and hurried across the California state line toward the Schuppin home. Responding to a call, the police overtook the van, and Tammy was released to the commune. On learning that the rescue had failed, Tammy's mother drove toward the shopping mall, hoping to see Tammy, but she was too late.

Tammy's three friends spent one night in jail on charges of kidnaping and assault and battery, but the charges were reduced to "unlawful restraint" and they were released on bail. Tammy's mother was charged with conspiracy to kidnap (for which she could have received a jail sentence) because she had helped plan the rescue. Other parents have been even less fortunate. In more than one instance the child, after rescue and escape, has filed a million-dollar lawsuit against the parents. Yet parents of Moon's followers are willing to take the risk and pay amounts up to 10 million dollars to have their children kidnaped and deprogramed, believing that this action is justified because the group's brainwashing techniques deprive their children of free choice. The

3. These groups are the Citizens' Freedom Foundation, P. O. Box 256, Chula Vista, CA 92010; Citizens Engaged in Reuniting Families, 252 Soundview Avenue, White Plains, NY 10606; and Return to Personal Choice, 1400 Commonwealth Avenue, West Newton, MA 02167.

extent to which the Unification Church brainwashes young people is illustrated in the following article.

Eighteen-year-old Wendy Helander led a well-rounded and carefree life. She was pretty, healthy, and bright enough to complete high school in less than four years. Her spare-time activities included cheerleading, ski trips, and sewing. "She had so much to offer," recalls her mother, "and her morals were so good; she was death against drugs and sex and anything like that."

As a college freshman, Wendy seemed a bit "confused" to her parents mainly because she became involved in Eastern religions and such exotic notions as reincarnation and World Soul. Looking back, Wendy described herself as a freshman: "I was an idealist, troubled by the suffering and violence in the world, searching for a meaningful life."

Wendy's New Messiah. When the telephone rang on Sunday evening, Wendy's mother knew her daughter was calling. But she hadn't expected the excitement in Wendy's voice. "We just had a magnificent weekend," Wendy kept repeating, "seeking guidance and discussing spiritual solutions to world problems with the most beautiful people!" Breathlessly, Wendy asked her mother, "And have *you* heard the *good news*?"

"*What* good news?" asked the startled Mrs. Helander. Wendy cheerfully responded, "The good news that there is a new Messiah on this earth!" Asked what she meant and where she was calling from, Wendy replied, "I've met some people who radiate so much love, so much warmth, and such caring that it's like I found a new family!"

When Wendy came home at Christmas, she kept telling her mother how happy she was although she cried a great deal of the time. She gave away all her most cherished possessions to friends of what she began calling the "Family." She dropped out of college and joined the Unification Church of Rev. Sun Myung Moon. Moving from city to city, Wendy began selling peanuts and carnations, soliciting contributions for a nonexistent youth ministry, a practice Rev. Moon calls "heavenly deceit." All the contributions, as much as $400 a day from each Moonie, are given to the church leader who lives in lush elegance while Wendy and her friends subsist on a meager allowance.

Lots of Lonely People. To understand such devotion, one must examine the methods used by the Unification Church to recruit and train its members. Clean-cut, always-smiling Moonies visit high school spots and college campuses to get young people into discussion about the critical condition of the world and moral values. As one Moonie recruiter reported, "There are lots of lonely people walking around."

Discussions always end with an invitation to hear a "most helpful" lecture at the nearest Unification Center. Recruiters rarely mention Rev. Moon or his church: they claim to belong to a Christian youth group. Following the lecture there is a dinner, and with the dinner comes a flurry of hearty friendship from the brothers and sisters of what soon becomes the "Family."

143

The next step for potential converts is a weekend worship at some secluded retreat. An exhausting and rigid schedule leaves little time for sleep. Special precautions are taken not to give inquirers time for private reflection. Recruits get a daily dose of six to eight hours of mind-numbing speeches and by the final day they learn that God has sent a new Messiah, Rev. Sun Myung Moon, to save the world—and them. From dawn until, well past midnight, days are crammed with group activities, calisthenics, sports, lots of singing and praying. Evenings are spent listening to Moonies testify how they have found peace, love, and joy in the family. Never left alone, recruits are encouraged to pour out their hearts to their new family, who offer constant attention and love. The weekend concludes with a hard-sell pitch for the next stage in the "conversion" process, an advanced seminar devoted to deeper truths.

Advanced seminars become more rigorous and life more spartan. Lectures, singing, praying, and body-conditioning keep recruits busy over eighteen hours each day. No time or opportunity is provided to phone or write relatives and friends. Then comes the pressure to join the Moon Family as full-time members. The recruits reach this moment of decision worn out from lack of sleep, numbed by endless speeches, cut off from family and friends, and charmed by the overwhelming warmth of the group. One convert recalls, "It was like being taken care of—the people were very friendly and you really thought they did love you." Another ex-Moonie remembers how "everybody was reinforcing each other all the time, and you just began to feel high. After seven days of fatiguing your body and manipulating your mind, they hook you, and you stay on."

Those attracted to Moon's church are often young people threatened by the outside world and confused, unable to face the frustrations of living on their own. Life in the Moonie commune offers a welcome refuge: no drugs, no drinks, no sex, no money, no problems, no choices, no decisions. (Rev. Moon even arranges periodic marriages without consultation!) From the team leader's cheerful "Rise and Shine" at 5:30 A.M. to the last group songs and prayers after midnight, Moonies rarely have to think for themselves. Surrounded by constantly smiling Moonies, they follow orders and perform assigned chores with enthusiasm.

An ex-Moonie who spent eight months in the movement said, "I'll tell you what attracted me. I saw people who looked happy at a time when I felt lonely and desperate." To such lonely people, Moon offers instant friendship and communion, a sense of belonging. To thousands of young people who feel threatened or frustrated, Moon's smiling family offers the security of perennial childhood. To insecure and fearful young people, Rev. Moon offers security, even assuring his followers, "I am your brain."[4]

Questions

1. The July 1976 issue of *Seventeen* magazine includes an article about cults. What advice does Jean Merrit, who heads "Return to Personal Choice," give for avoiding entrapment by the cults?

4. "Sun Myung Moon," *Landmarks* (volume 4, number 10). Copyright 1977, 1980 by the Board of Publications of the Christian Reformed Church.

2. List any evidence you can find that the First Unification Church brainwashes its members.
3. Suppose you met a Moonie selling flowers and soliciting contributions. How would you respond? What is the best way for a Christian to respond?
4. Read Matthew 24:5–12. Of what time is Jesus speaking? How does this explain the success of Sun Myung Moon?
5. Within the First Unification Church, members need to make few, if any, decisions. Why does this fact appeal to some people?
6. Read II Peter 2:1–3 in several translations. Make a list that describes the effect false leaders or prophets have on people. How does your list compare with the effect Moon has had on his followers?

Additional Sources of Information

Edwards, Christopher. *Crazy for God*. Englewood Cliffs, NJ: Prentice-Hall, 1979.
An ex-Moonie describes the seven months that transformed him from an independent Yale graduate to a totally submissive Moon disciple. The epilogue describes his kidnaping and deprograming.

McBeth, Leon. *Strange New Religions*. Nashville: Broadman, 1977.
This book contains chapters about the Unification Church, Hare Krishna, Zen Buddhism, and other religions that attract American youth. The author tells where they came from, what they teach, and who is attracted to them.

Stoner, Carroll, and Parke, Jo Anne. *All God's Children: The Cult Experience—Salvation or Slavery*. New York: Penguin, 1979.
The authors, both newspaper editors, share their research and personal experience with cults such as the Unification Church, Hare Krishna, Divine Light

Mission, and others. Recruiting methods, teachings, and deprograming are discussed.

Yamamoto, J. Isamu. *The Puppet Master: An Inquiry into Sun Myung Moon and the Unification Church*. Downers Grove, IL: Inter-Varsity, 1977.
The author, from the Spiritual Counterfeits Projects of Berkeley, California, gives an interesting account of Moon, his church, its members, and its teachings.

6

The Way International

The seal of The Way International depicts the group's slogan, "The Word Over the World." The tree in the bottom half of the circle represents the structure of The Way International.

The Way International began in the midwestern United States only a few decades ago. Disclaiming the label of "church," The Way identifies itself as a Bible research organization. Yet the group ordains clergy, holds Bible-study fellowship meetings in homes, sends out missionaries, commemorates the Lord's Supper, and sponsors conferences for members.

Although The Way International was established in the 1950s, rapid growth did not begin until 1968, when young people, many disillusioned by the institutional church, began to join The Way by the thousands. The Way does not release official membership statistics, but membership is estimated at more than 50,000. Active throughout the United States, The Way has sent scores of young missionaries into thirty-four other countries. The group's goal is to enroll more than a million inquirers in its special Bible study course by 1990. In this chapter, we will examine briefly

The Way's history and beliefs, as well as the elements that attract young people to the movement.

The Origin of The Way International

Victor Paul Wierwille, born in 1917, prepared for the ministry after a strict fundamentalist upbringing. After high school, he attended the Moody Bible Institute and the University of Chicago Divinity School. He also received his Master of Theology degree from Princeton Seminary and a Doctor of Theology degree from Pike's Peak Seminary. Ordained as a minister in the Evangelical and Reformed Church, Wierwille served a number of congregations. However, his early years in the ministry proved disturbing; the more he studied various religious ideas, the more unsure he became. According to Wierwille, he kept his doubts to himself until he received a direct revelation from God, informing him that he had been chosen to restore the pure teachings of the Bible. As he prayed about his confused state of mind, God allegedly spoke to him, audibly informing him that he would be given the true meaning of the Bible as it had not been known since the first century, on the condition that he would teach it to others. Circumstances prevented Wierwille from speaking publicly of his experience; he assumed that members of his church would disapprove. Meanwhile, however, his inner struggle mounted, until finally he sought to resolve his doubts.

When he was in his early thirties, Wierwille

burned his library—every commentary, theological book, and religious encyclopedia—every book except the Bible. He resolved to study the Bible alone, without the aid of human interpretation. After several years, Wierwille developed his personal interpretation of the Bible which, he claimed, was a recovery of the true doctrines which had been lost to the church since the time of the apostles. During this time, he experienced a deep spiritual renewal characterized by a victorious, joyful outlook on life, and an ability to speak in tongues. Wierwille's newly-discovered beliefs and biblical interpretations became the substance of his lecture series, called Power for Abundant Living.

In 1957, at age forty, Wierwille resigned his position in the Evangelical and Reformed Church in Van Wert, Ohio, so that he could devote all his time to teaching the Power for Abundant Living (PFAL) course. Within a few years, he had established the headquarters of The Way International on his family's farm in New Knoxville, Ohio. He launched a series of lecture tours that took him throughout the United States, traveling at first by motorcycle and later using a Bible Research bus. As the movement grew, The Way acquired a college in Emporia, Kansas, and established a publishing house, the American Christian Press. To mark the twentieth anniversary of the founding of The Way, Wierwille publicly identified himself as God's chosen reformer. On Reformation Day, 1977, Wierwille marched to a New Knoxville, Ohio, church and nailed his theses on the door.

His statements primarily rejected the Trinity and the deity of Jesus Christ.

The rapid expansion and development of The Way International has manifested Wierwille's dynamic personality. Those who meet Wierwille find him an impressive person, always well-dressed and flashing a smile. Affectionately known as "the Doctor," Wierwille possesses such personal charm that his followers gladly travel hundreds of miles to attend state conferences where he lectures. Some members of The Way regard Wierwille as the greatest prophet since Jeremiah. His dynamic personality takes on special significance in the PFAL course, which consists of thirty-six hours of videotaped lectures by Wierwille, shown to prospective members in three-hour segments.

The Way International uses the analogy of a tree for its organization. The *trunk* is the international headquarters in New Knoxville, Ohio; the *limbs* are the state organizations; the *branches* are the organizations in cities; the *twigs* are the home or campus Bible-study groups; the *leaves* are the individual members.

Beliefs of The Way International

The teachings of The Way are found in the following books by Wierwille: *Jesus Christ Is Not God, The Bible Tells Me So, The Word's Way*, and *Receiving the Holy Spirit Today*. A study of these sources reveals the essential differences between the beliefs of The Way and those of historic Christianity.

The Nature of God

Because Wierwille relies heavily on the Bible and because he teaches that the early church correctly understood the nature of God, The Way agrees with orthodox Christianity that God is Spirit, that He is the Creator of all things, that He is eternal, and that He is personal. However, claiming that the church assimilated pagan beliefs during the third and fourth centuries, Wierwille denies the Trinity and the deity of Christ. Hence, The Way views God as one in substance and one in person; He is the Father, and no more than the Father. To uncover the significance of this view, let us note four teachings of The Way relating to the nature of God.

God alone exists from all eternity. In *Jesus Christ Is Not God*, Wierwille makes a sharp distinction between God and the Word of God (John 1:1–2). He explains that the *Word* or *Idea* of God is not the same as God. Just as an idea, in human terms, is not the same as a brain, so the Word of God is not synonymous with God. Note how Wierwille develops the meaning of the Word to maintain his point.

Before creation, the Word existed in God's foreknowledge. Therefore, Wierwille says, Christ existed before creation only in the sense that the Word existed in the mind of God. After God created the world, He orally communicated His Word to Adam, Noah, the patriarchs, and others before

153

written records were made. Later, as historical records were kept, God gave His written Word, the Old Testament. From Abraham's time to the close of the Old Testament, God's Word came in written form through prophets, historians, psalmists, and other writers of Scripture. Finally, the Word of God was incarnated in the person of Jesus of Nazareth. According to The Way, Jesus was a more advanced, concrete expression of the Word of God, but was distinct from and independent of God—so independent that Wierwille developed the popular slogan, "If Jesus is God, we are not saved." According to The Way, God could not remain God if He became Jesus.

Since the death and resurrection of Jesus, God has communicated the Word by dwelling within the believer. The "indwelling Word" is granted to individual believers who are baptized by the Holy Spirit. In summary, Wierwille teaches that the Word, distinct from God, has existed in these phases: in the mind of God before creation; in oral expression from God; in written form from God; fleshed out in Jesus; and within the believer.

Jesus is the Son of God, but not God the Son. Carefully note the following logical progression in the teachings of The Way, resulting in a denial of the deity of Jesus. First of all, Jesus didn't exist prior to His incarnation; only the Word (Idea) existed. God implanted His Word into a miraculously conceived human being, Jesus, through His mother Mary. Because Jesus was divinely implanted when Mary conceived, He was born sinless. Because of His obedience, Jesus became the Son of God, but He is not God the Son, says

Wierwille. Although The Way claims that Jesus is Savior and Redeemer, He may not (and this is the crucial part) be worshiped, for worship is due only to God. The authority and supernatural power which characterized Jesus' ministry were derived from His baptism, as we will note below, not from His authority as God the Son. In summary, Jesus was a sinless human person, distinct from and independent of God, not to be worshiped.

The Holy Spirit is not regarded as a person, but as synonymous with God the Father. Because the Father is *Holy* and because the father is a *Spirit*, He may be referred to as the *Holy Spirit*. According to Wierwille, this is the only correct way to speak of the Holy Spirit, using capital letters. It is not correct to say that Christians receive the Holy Spirit. What believers receive is holy spirit (without capital letters), because believers receive an energy, not a divine person. Because God and the Holy Spirit are synonymous, not distinct persons, The Way insists that the two sentences "The Father gives the holy spirit," and "The Holy Spirit gives the holy spirit" express the same thing. Although we will pursue this further, we can conclude at this point that The Way rejects the doctrine of the Trinity, denies the unique, separate personality of the Holy Spirit, and reinterprets the biblical teaching that believers received the Holy Spirit. We will conclude our study of the nature of God by noting a final feature of The Way's teaching.

God exists, according to The Way, for the express purpose of pleasing and empowering members of The Way International. Based on a study of their literature and the role of God in their personal testimonies, we conclude that they consider God as One whose sole purpose and supreme work is to grant victorious living and miraculous power to followers of The Way. Perhaps this view results from their belief that previous expressions of the Word (spoken Word, written Word, incarnate Word) do not apply directly to our lives today; only Paul's letters and the Acts of the Apostles pertain. Regardless of the reason, The Way neglects the exalted God of the Old Testament and the Psalms, and refuses to recognize the gracious God who lovingly executes His plan of redemption. Instead, the only work of God featured in The Way's ministry is the imparting of the holy spirit, which enables The Way followers to do the same work that Christ did. After meeting personally with Wierwille, Allen A. Denton wrote,

> What troubles me theologically is not so much [The Way's] belief about Christ, for it can easily be proved heretical, but rather the cult's view of God, which holds that God is bound by its teaching and is responsible to see that each Way follower is blessed. The holiness, mystery and majesty of God are all missing in The Way's teaching.[1]

As we have seen, The Way denies the Trinity, rejects the deity of Christ, dismisses the person-

1. "Uproar in Emporia," *The Christian Century*, May 31, 1978, p. 589. At the time of this interview, Denton was pastor of a Presbyterian church in Emporia, Kansas, home of The Way College.

ality of the Holy Spirit, and limits the glory and power of God. Consider now in greater detail the role of Christ in The Way's teaching.

Christ and the Human Problem

As we observed earlier, Dr. Wierwille teaches that Jesus lived a sinless life, and that He died and was resurrected. He also teaches that Jesus ascended into heaven and will return again. But The Way's view of Christ's role in salvation differs substantially from Christian teachings. Although the two are closely intertwined, we will first look at Christ's role and then apply that understanding to our spiritual problem and its solution.

Wierwille teaches that Jesus Christ was a sinless human being who became the Son of God by virtue of His obedient life. However, being sinless and obedient supplied Jesus with less power than He needed to work miracles and become our Savior. For this reason, Jesus received a human holy spirit at His baptism, which enabled Him to launch His ministry of healing, teaching, raising the dead, and giving His life on the cross. According to followers of The Way, the most important and useful thing Christ did occurred after He ascended into heaven. Only then did He give this same gift, a human holy spirit, to His disciples. This gift enabled them to speak in tongues, perform miracles, raise the dead, and heal the sick—in brief, to duplicate His ministry. To further understand this, we must examine the human spiritual problem.

According to The Way, the human spiritual

problem is this: As a result of Adam's fall, humanity lost both the *image of God* and *spirit*. Everyone since Adam has lacked both and has been born only as flesh, nothing more. By believing in Christ, however, a person can regain what Adam had originally, the same gift which the disciples received at Pentecost—a human holy spirit. Speaking in tongues signals the arrival of a human holy spirit in the life of the believer. Once this happens, a believer is no longer flesh alone, but flesh and spirit. In other words, receiving a human holy spirit is to the believer what baptism was to Jesus. The Way teaches that as a result, the person who receives a human holy spirit can do the works of Jesus, and even greater works than He did (John 14:12).

Speaking in tongues is evidence to The Way believers that a human holy spirit has been given to an inquirer, and that he or she possesses power for abundant living that resembles the power of Christ. The believer is enabled to do what Jesus did—attain sinless perfection, perfect health, happiness, and success. In fact, gifts of healing and even resurrection from the dead are reported among followers of The Way. To the degree that believers practice speaking in tongues, they will be able to develop power to heal, to prophesy, to interpret, to raise from the dead—in brief, to lead lives of abundant moral, physical, and spiritual power. Any person who focuses faith on events prior to Pentecost lacks the power for abundant living; what happened prior to Pentecost belongs to an obsolete phase of history, according to The

Way. Pentecost is the great event and the role of Jesus makes it possible for sinful persons to receive the gift of a human holy spirit.

As additional information about The Way becomes available, new dimensions of the power for abundant living come into public view. For example, there is evidence that The Way teaches that once a person has received the human holy spirit, he or she no longer sins. This is strongly suggested in an interview with two former members of The Way International. Note the following excerpt from that interview:

Q. While you were in The Way, did you find them trying to give you advice or guidance on areas of morality, or sex?
A. I was very young at the time. They used sex in the wrong way, in whatever way they wanted to.
Q. Were they into "free sex"?
A. Yes, with whomever you want. They condoned it. They said God condoned it, that you can sleep with any man and get away with it.
Q. What was their justification for condoning this?
A. They tell you that you can have free sex or do your own thing because you are born again and going to heaven. So, you can't commit adultery.[2]

To what degree this interview complies with the official teachings of The Way will become more clear as other defectors speak out. Much of The

2. Joel A. MacCollam, " 'The Way' Seemed Right But the End Thereof . . .: An Interview with Two Cult Defectors," *Eternity*, 27 (November 1977), p. 26.

Way's teaching is based on Wierwille's personal interpretation of the Bible, and we will conclude our study by looking at his understanding.

The Bible

I related earlier that Wierwille destroyed his entire library after God allegedly told him that a new and correct interpretation of the Bible would be restored. This new, restored gospel is included in the teachings of The Way International and rests on two central assumptions about the Bible.

First, Wierwille claims that most of the Bible pertains to an outdated period of sacred history. Only the epistles of Paul (and perhaps the Acts of the Apostles) apply to Christians today, according to The Way. All other parts of the Bible, including the Gospels, belong to a pre-Pentecost period. These records of sacred history have been superseded or preempted by the current period of sacred history, beginning with Pentecost. For all practical purposes, The Way dismisses most of the Bible as irrelevant.

Second, The Way followers are drilled in Wierwille's interpretation of many passages of the Bible and believe that these are *essential* to a correct understanding of the Bible. In other words, The Way claims that a second authority, the teaching of Wierwille, is required to correctly understand the Bible. This second authority, inspired directly by God, is certainly indispensable, if not equal to the Bible! We may conclude that Wierwille has determined for The Way members both what constitutes the revealed Word of God and the meaning of the Bible itself.

Perhaps the fundamental error of The Way is its acceptance of an authority outside the Bible which dictates what the Bible teaches. Once Wierwille's teachings were accepted, they became the real bible of The Way International, and faith in the Word of God was replaced by faith in Victor Paul Wierwille.

Recruitment Methods of The Way

Two of the most effective methods for recruiting inquirers are invitations (posted on bulletin boards) to Way meetings and personal contacts by Way members. In either method, the initial contact makes some attention-getting claim. Since The Way seeks primarily to reach young people, members often invite prospective members to their meetings through advertisements on college bulletin boards. On one campus, invitations to the meetings appeared with striking slogans such as: "You can have POWER for abundant living!" "Jesus Christ is NOT God," "You can kick the FEAR AND WORRY HABIT," and "God has stopped making BALONEY!" These invitations are, of course, intended to attract persons who have not discovered spiritual assurance.

Way members employ the same arresting approach in personal contacts. One student reported that she was studying alone in the college commons when two Way members approached her:

> One of them asked me, "Do you believe God still works miracles?" Not knowing what was going on, I simply replied, "Sure, I think He does." No sooner had I spoken the words than he responded, "Well, I KNOW He can because I've seen it happen!" He proceeded to tell me how involvement in The Way had given him new power, motivation, and spiritual energy. "I used to be into drugs heavy," he claimed, "and now God has given me victory. I used to be bitter and hate people, but now I love everybody. I used to wander around in a daze, but now I've found a *real* purpose in life." After elaborating a bit more, he invited me to attend the next meeting of the campus twig.

Obviously, arousing curiosity about The Way, whether by poster or personal contact, seems to be the primary method used by the organization. If a positive response occurs, The Way recruiters enter a second phase.

When a person accepts an invitation to attend or shows up at a twig meeting, he or she becomes the object of concentrated attention, which The Way members refer to as *undershepherding*. This lavish display of affection raises the inquirer's expectations and reinforces positive attitudes toward the group. Lee Reppik (a pseudonym) reported his personal experience, which both illustrates the lure of undershepherding and introduces us to the nature of twig meetings.

> When I was invited to attend a twig meeting, I accepted, mainly because I was going through some

hard times and I felt a need for some moral support. No sooner had I accepted than a barrage of attention began. Phone calls and personal notes by mail told me how pleased everyone in the group was that I planned to attend. So I eagerly drove up to this attractive home in the suburbs on a Thursday evening. Greeted warmly, I was quickly introduced to the members of the twig, all positive and cheerful people. Some identified themselves as the ones who had phoned or sent notes. Everyone was enthusiastic, clean-cut, and happy. After introductions, the Bible study began, under the leadership of a visiting teacher who had received advanced training at The Way College in Emporia, Kansas. Verse by verse he explained the second chapter of Philippians, often referring to Greek words and their *true meaning*. Repeatedly he said, "People used to think this meant something else, but a study of the original Greek by Dr. Wierwille reveals the true, hidden meaning." I soon learned that this group believed their interpretation of the Bible was different from what I had learned in catechism, and that they not only regarded their teachings to be better—they claimed to have the *true meaning of the Bible*! Although I was suspicious of their teachings, it was an impressive sight to observe a group of cheerful, confident people studying the Bible.

After the Bible study, the host explained, a period of ten or fifteen minutes was set aside for any "manifestation of the Holy Spirit," during which we would all sit silently waiting for the Father to bless us. After a few minutes, the silence was broken by a young man who was speaking in a series of strange, unintelligible words which sounded to me like Chinese. The host asked if anyone had the gift to interpret what had been said, and almost immediately someone offered an interpretation that went something like this: "You are my children," says our Father, "and you alone have received my glory so that others may see my glory in you. As you walk through life, show forth my glory which I have given you. And I will be at your side, because you are my dear and glory-filled children." Four times during this quiet period people spoke in heavenly languages, as they called them, and each time the language sounded different. Yet all the interpretations were similar, affirming that we, the twig, were God's unique children who were loved in some special, personal way.

Delighted by all of this, my host walked me out to my car, his face still shining with enthusiasm. I, too, he promised, could learn to speak in heavenly languages by taking a course called Power for Abundant Living. After twelve classes, he assured me, I would be given a heavenly language, along with new power to lead a more victorious life.

As I drove home, reflecting on these experiences, two observations struck me. First of all, I had seldom, if ever, shown such open acceptance and enthusiasm toward visitors or members of my church, which I determined to do in the future. Second, my experience convinced me beyond doubt that any person with unmet spiritual and social needs, of any age, would have a difficult time resisting the acceptance and positive atmosphere of a twig meeting.

As Lee's experience indicates, the goal of undershepherding is to enroll inquirers in the

Power for Abundant Living course, after which hopefully they will become full-fledged members of The Way.

The Power for Abundant Living Course

The PFAL course is of central importance to The Way International. Anyone who shows the slightest interest in The Way is urged to take the course. No one can become a member without taking it. The PFAL course features Wierwille in twelve videotaped sessions, each approximately three hours long. The course is usually offered four nights a week for three weeks at a cost of about eighty-five dollars. Those who enroll are guaranteed answers to ninety-five percent of their questions about the Bible and everything else. Once the initial tuition is paid, one can take the course repeatedly at no additional cost.

An inquirer who viewed the three-hour sessions describes the course:

Four nights a week we got together for the course, watching the videotapes of Dr. Wierwille. We were not allowed to talk, to take notes, or to ask questions. We were told to concentrate one hundred percent on the dynamic and enthusiastic presentations. Night after night we learned how the Bible is supposed to be read and understood. Powerful speeches and airtight logic combined to teach us that Jesus Christ is not God, that the Trinity came from pagan beliefs, that the Holy Spirit should be spelled as the holy spirit, and that the true meaning of the Bible, lost to all churches, has now been restored through Dr. Wierwille. Over and over he emphasized, "The Bible means what it says and says what it means," "The Bible fits like hand in glove," and "The Word of God is the Will of God." After spending thirty-six hours listening to and watching Wierwille's powerful, charismatic presentation, bombarded by his slogans and beliefs, it all seemed to make sense.

The highlight of the PFAL course came in the final session when the Doctor taught us how to speak in tongues, explaining that speaking in tongues is required for any person who is born again, because spirit baptism has replaced water baptism and one must be baptized to be saved. We were instructed to sit quietly and follow his instructions exactly. He then gave us breathing exercises consisting of inhaling and exhaling rhythmically, followed by instructions to move our lips, throats, and tongues. Soon people responded with the exciting sounds of "heavenly languages." That's the real clincher for most people. At the end of the last session, everyone in our group, including me, had been overpowered by the teachings, techniques, and dynamism of Dr. Wierwille.

Those who complete the PFAL course by speaking in a "heavenly language" are confirmed as converts, having been baptized "by the holy spirit." Converts are urged to spread Wierwille's teachings in a variety of ways. Some work to establish new Bible-study groups, in a program called Word Over the World (WOW). Some become WOW ambassadors on a part-time basis, while others leave school and full-time jobs to become Way missionaries. Those with musical talent can join one of The Way's musical groups, "The Joyful Noise" or "The Good Seed." These groups go on tour and offer "Rock of Ages Festivals." Young converts are encouraged to attend The Way College, which features summer outreach programs such as the Minuteman Program, in which students set up twigs in assigned cities and enroll people in the PFAL course. Before their senior year, students must spend a full year as Way ambassadors in Canada, the United States, or one of thirty-three other countries. Wherever they go, members of The Way earn a reputation for being enthusiastic and committed. They freely and openly testify that God has transformed them spiritually.

Questions

1. Do you think young people would be as attracted to The Way meetings if the fellowship in their own churches were more intimate? Why or why not?
2. After warning against false teachings, Jude speaks of different attitudes toward those who follow false teachings (vv. 17–23). Use commentaries to learn what these verses mean. What does this passage tell us about relating to The Way members? Does it justify using force to rescue Christians who come under The Way's influence?
3. Wierwille often claims, "The Bible is the greatest how-to-do-it book ever written." Do you agree or disagree with this claim? Why or why not?
4. Lee Reppik reports that members of the twig he attended never established any contact with him after

he left the group. After this experience, Reppik concluded, "They sought to pressure me into believing what they believe. Acceptance was conditional—only if I agreed with them would they accept me. That wasn't love—it was manipulation." Do you think this is an accurate evaluation?

5. In John 14:16–17, 26, II Corinthians 13:14, and Ephesians 4:30, the Holy Spirit is mentioned. Review these passages and analyze how the Bible contradicts The Way's teaching about the Holy Spirit.

6. Two popular groups, First Unification Church and The Way, have arisen in the mid-twentieth century. What social and spiritual conditions might explain this?

Additional Sources of Information

Boa, Kenneth. *Cults, World Religions, and You*. Wheaton, IL: Victor, 1977.

Enroth, Ronald H. *Youth, Brainwashing, and the Extremist Cults*. Grand Rapids: Zondervan, 1977.
This book has chapters about The Way, The Unification Church, the Hare Krishna movement, and other groups that have been accused of brainwashing. In the first section, Enroth describes each of these cults, using case histories. In the second section, he analyzes why the cults are popular.

7

A Summary

Each of the five groups discussed in this book is unique; each has its own history, beliefs, and practices. But as we noted at the outset, certain characteristics are common to all—namely, an unbiblical view of salvation, denial of the deity of Christ, and a claim of new revelation. We have included Table 1 to present in concise form the characteristics of each group and to help you review what you've read in this book.

Table 1

	Founder/ Origin	Beliefs	
		The Nature of God	The Person and Work of Christ
Jehovah's Witnesses	Charles Taze Russell (1852–1916), captivated by the Second Adventists' logical analysis of biblical prophecies, spread the insights he claimed by lecturing and writing.	Jehovah is a spirit and the creator of the world, but He is *not* a trinity. Only the name *Jehovah* may be used for God. Only Jehovah may receive honor and praise.	Christ left his pre-earth life to assume a fully human form. He was Jehovah's Son, a perfect human being. He was raised a spirit creature. His death was a human sacrifice, making it possible for some to be saved. He returned invisibly in 1914.
The Church of Jesus Christ of Latter-day Saints	Joseph Smith (1805–1844) lived in New York State during a time of great religious turbulence. He claimed many revelations and the discovery of golden plates from which the *Book of Mormon* resulted.	God was once human. By a series of progressions He became God. He has a body of flesh and bone. He is not a trinity; the Holy Spirit is an impersonal force, and Christ is united with the Father in purpose only. Many lesser gods exist.	Christ is the firstborn spirit-child of God. He created earth under the direction of the Father. His death gives all believers immortality, but the reward of life in heaven depends on each individual's obedience. Therefore Christ's death makes possible, but does not assure, salvation.
Christian Science	Mary Baker Eddy (1821–1910) suffered poor health and religious confusion. After experiencing a "divine healing" in 1866, she consolidated her thoughts into a faith centered on belief in spiritual healing.	God is a divine Principle, an impersonal Absolute. Nothing exists in reality which is not God. God is Love, Mind, Truth. He is not triune. The Old Testament Jehovah was a tribal God of war; Jesus revealed God as a Principle of Love; the Holy Comforter is Christian Science.	Teachings about Christ are elusive and ambiguous. He became human so that he would appear in a form mortals could perceive, but he was not God and man united. He was not divine. He seemed to suffer and die but actually did not. He unveiled the spiritual idea of divine Love.

The Way of Salvation	The Bible	Distinctive Practices	Organization
Christ made it possible for human beings to attain eternal life by following the way of Jehovah. By honoring Jehovah purely and following Christ's example of obedience, people can escape annihilation.	The Bible is God's infallible, inspired Word, but the only pure translation is the *New World Translation*, based on Russell's insights. The Witnesses misinterpret many verses, because they fail to consider context.	The Witnesses' desire to imitate Christ's obedience produces lives and families of strong moral character. Witnesses disapprove of birthday and holiday celebrations and refuse blood transfusions.	Headquarters of the hierarchical structure are in Brooklyn, New York. Every baptized convert is a minister, expected to preach and witness. The Witnesses are aggressive evangelists.
At the final judgment, all will be resurrected and will receive exaltation according to their devotion and obedience in their earthly lives. Immortality results from faith in Christ, but exaltation results from good works.	The information in the Bible is obsolete and full of errors which crept into various translations. The Mormons have many other scriptures that resulted from new revelations. These revelations continue through the First Presidency.	Mormons baptize children at age eight. They also practice baptism for the dead. Devout couples may obtain celestial marriages. Mormons are known for their devotion, obedience, high moral standards, and strong family life.	The hierarchical structure includes a prophet, twelve apostles, and the priesthood. The president receives continuing revelation. The Mormon church is experiencing phenomenal growth. Church offices and the Mormon Tabernacle are located in Salt Lake City, Utah.
Sin does not exist; it is an illusion of mortal mind. Salvation (deliverance from every form of evil) comes by right thinking and a correct comprehension of God. We deliver ourselves from sin and sickness by realizing they don't exist.	The Bible can be understood only with its "unerring and divine" companion book, *Science and Health*, by Mary Baker Eddy. To read the Bible correctly, we must eliminate its material elements, which reproduce the messages of mortal mind.	Baptism and the Lord's Supper are recognized but seen as daily, individual experiences. Devout Christian Scientists refuse all medical treatment, believing that healing comes by denying the false messages of illness.	Sunday worship services are conducted by readers. The mother church is located in Boston, Massachusetts. Each local congregation provides a reading room in its area. Christian Scientists are not aggressive evangelists.

	Founder/ Origin	Beliefs	
		The Nature of God	The Person and Work of Christ
First Unification Church	Sun Myung Moon (b. 1920) grew up in a Korean village. He claimed that Jesus appeared to him and told him that he had been selected to complete Christ's work. God revealed a new set of teachings to him.	God is a Creator whose plans have been repeatedly foiled by Satan. Rev. Moon is the new messiah who will restore relations between God and man. Moon is God in visible form.	Jesus was the second Adam. He effected spiritual salvation through His death, but failed to accomplish the physical salvation of humanity (by fathering God's family on earth). Therefore a new messiah, Moon, is needed to bring physical salvation. Jesus was not God. Moon is God.
The Way International	Victor Paul Wierwille (b. 1917) was reared as a strict fundamentalist. He became a minister, but was deeply troubled by doubts. Then God revealed that he had been chosen to restore the pure gospel. He burned his library, resigned from ministry, and began the PFAL course.	God is Spirit. He created all things. He is personal and eternal. He is not triune. The Holy Spirit is synonymous with the Father. God exists for the express purpose of pleasing and empowering members of The Way International.	Christ was a sinless man who became God's son because of His obedient life. He received a human holy spirit at His baptism, which enabled Him to work miracles and give His life. He was divinely begotten and is our savior, but He is distinct from God (He is not God) and is *not* to be worshiped.

The Way of Salvation	The Bible	Distinctive Practices	Organization
Moon may forgive sin. He is also the mediator through whom members pray to the Heavenly Father. Salvation comes by rebirth to sinlessness, through Father and Mother Moon.	The teachings are contained in *Divine Principle*, Moon's bible. The Bible is not truth itself, but a textbook for finding the truth. It must not be accepted as absolute in every detail.	The group is best-known for its deceptive and aggressive solicitation and recruitment methods. The church has been accused of brainwashing and mind control. Moonies are clean-cut and smiling, but often look like zombies.	Church offices are located in New York City. The church owns property throughout the United States. Members of the "Family" meet at local Unification Centers. Moon rarely addresses his followers.
In Adam's fall, humanity lost both the image of God and spirit. Humans are born as flesh only. But by belief in Jesus, they can receive a human holy spirit. This gift is indicated by a person's ability to speak in tongues.	Only the letters of Paul (and perhaps the Book of Acts) apply to believers today. The rest of the Bible is obsolete and irrelevant. Wierwille's teaching is necessary to understand the parts of the Bible that are relevant today.	The Way aggressively recruits college students. Members use full acceptance and warmth to manipulate inquirers. Recruits take the PFAL course. Converts speak in tongues. The Way advocates free sex.	The Way identifies itself as a Bible-research organization. The group ordains clergy, sends out missionaries, observes the Lord's Supper, and holds member conferences. Bible-study groups (twigs) meet in members' homes. Headquarters are in New Knoxville, Ohio.